Advance Praise for

GLASS CEILINGS and BOTTOMLESS PITS

"Randy Albelda and Chris Tilly have produced another in a long line of engaging and enlightening texts. *Glass Ceilings and Bottomless Pits* provides useful data, pointed arguments, and wise advice about moving forward."

—Linda Chavez-Thompson
Executive Vice-President, AFL-CIO

"Welfare reform has been shaped by a set of myths about women, work, and poverty. Randy Albelda and Chris Tilly successfully refute these myths in *Glass Ceilings and Bottomless Pits,* with their comprehensive review of the status of working women on the bottom and on the top. This analysis is sensitive to the ways that race and class can fracture the women's movement. More importantly, Albelda and Tilly move beyond standard problem analysis to offer both policy solutions and suggestions for implementing those solutions."

—Julianne Malveaux,
economist, syndicated columnist, and author,
Sex, Lies & Stereotypes: Perspectives of a Mad Economist

"Every activist and advocate working for justice for low-income women should read this book. Albelda and Tilly give us the documentation and analysis to back up what we already know is true: the economic system isn't working for poor women, and welfare 'reform' is making matters much worse. How wonderful to hear from economists who are based in reality!"

—Diane Dujon, co-editor, *For Crying Out Loud:
Women's Poverty in the United States,*
and member, National Welfare Rights Union

GLASS CEILINGS
and BOTTOMLESS PITS:

Women's Work,
Women's Poverty

by **RANDY ALBELDA**
and **CHRIS TILLY**

with an appendix by
Dorothy K. Seavey

South End Press
Boston, MA

HV
95
.A5988
1997

Cover design by Beth Fortune
Text design by Sheila Walsh
Printed in the USA

Library of Congress Cataloging-in-Publication Data
Albelda, Randy Pearl.
    Glass ceilings and bottomless pits : women's work, women's poverty
/ by Randy Albelda and Chris Tilly.
        p.   cm.
    Includes index.
    ISBN 0-89608-566-X. — ISBN 0-89608-565-1 (pbk.)
    1. Public welfare—United States. 2. Poor women—United States.
3. Welfare recipients—United States. 4. United States—Social
policy—1993-   I. Tilly, Chris. II. Title.
HV95.A5988   1997
362.83'086'942—dc21   97-17419
                                                           CIP

South End Press, 116 Saint Botolph Street, Boston, MA 02115
03 02 01 00 99 98 97   1 2 3 4 5 6 7

® GCIU 745-C

To Mary and Marie

Contents

List of Figures

List of Tables

Acknowledgments

This volume builds on a booklet we wrote about women and poverty in Massachusetts in 1994.[1] In that project, we were supported by the Poverty and Race Research Action Council to work directly with the Massachusetts Women's Statewide Legislative Network (WSLN). The grant was to help link academics with public policy practitioners concerned with racial and economic inequality. During 1994 and 1995, we toured the state of Massachusetts with WSLN's executive director, Kelly Bates, speaking about welfare reform and women's poverty. The response was very positive, and the booklet has been used by students, advocates, and legislators around the state. This book is expanded well beyond the scope of the original booklet and includes "nationalized" and updated data, as well as far more extensive political analysis.

A variety of people have given us financial, intellectual, and moral support. The Russell Sage Foundation provided support for Chris Tilly during part of the time spent writing this book. The University of Massachusetts at Boston and at Lowell provided funds for research assistance.

Diane Balser, founding executive director of the WSLN, wrote the original proposal and has worked hard to expand women's political agendas to include a variety of economic issues. We thank her for her continued perseverance and commitment. Kelly Bates, the subsequent director, carried on the organization's strong commitment to low-income women's empowerment, and has been a constant supporter of our work. Steve

Savner at the Center for Law and Social Policy and Deborah Harris at the Massachusetts Law Reform Institute deserve enormous credit for many of the ideas in this book. They provided resources on current state and national policy proposals on welfare reform, as well as constructive suggestions all along the way. For helpful ongoing discussions on poverty and welfare reform, we thank Diane Dujon, Nancy Folbre, Marie Kennedy, Mary Lassen, Cindy Mann, Ann Withorn, the members of Massachusetts Academics' Working Group on Poverty, and our students at the University of Massachusetts at Boston and at Lowell. We also thank Ed Besozzi, Urska Cvek, Laurie Dougherty, Paula Maher, Tiffany Manuel, Cheryl Seleski, and Hong Xu for their research assistance, and Sheila Walsh for her design and production skills. Our South End Press editors, Cynthia Peters and Lynn Lu, provided insightful feedback and helped greatly in sharpening and "packaging" our message. For continued love and support in all our endeavors, we thank our families, and in particular our soul mates, Mary Eich and Marie Kennedy.

Notes

1. *Glass Ceilings and Bottomless Pits: Women, Income, and Poverty in Massachusetts* (Boston: Women's Statewide Legislative Network, 1994).

Introduction

When writing a book, it is generally gratifying to find that actual events are making that book ever more relevant. This is one book, however, we would rather have seen become *less* relevant. True, the main subjects of the book are not likely to soon fade in importance in the United States; women's job market disadvantages, lopsided responsibility for childcare, and disproportionate poverty pose long-term problems. But as we began writing, we hoped that the nation would find the insight, empathy, and political will to move toward more constructive solutions than currently exist.

That has not happened. Instead, the debate on poverty and welfare has grown more irrational, shrill, and mean-spirited. Biased and inaccurate perceptions of women, people of color, and poor people have distorted the public discussion. First many state legislatures and then both Congress and President Clinton approved laws that, despite a rhetoric of encouraging self-reliance, in practice punish rather than aid poor families.

The new laws are already wreaking severe consequences, starting with the millions of women who currently—or until recently—relied on welfare programs. But the impact does not end there. We argue in this book that the turn toward harsher welfare policies has created negative political and economic spillovers for *all* women and their families.

In this environment, our initial purposes for writing the book have taken on additional urgency. We hope to change the terms of the debate around poverty and welfare in the United States, by pointing out the connections between poverty and the work/family stresses faced by all families. We would especially like this book to be used by women and women's groups, because so much is at stake in the lives of women and children.

What's in this book

We start with the basic facts about women and poverty in the economy and build a bridge from there to analysis, policy, and strategy. Chapter One highlights the big changes affecting women in the U.S. economy and summarizes the book's arguments and policy recommendations. In Chapter Two, we describe who's poor—and who isn't—in the United States and examine how poverty has come to be defined. Chapter Three puts wealth and poverty back in a *family* context, describing the different types of families in the United States and tracing their economic fortunes. In Chapter Four, we examine why women do so much worse, in terms of access and earnings, than men in the workforce, and in Chapter Five, we zero in on the forces that trap so many single mothers in poverty.

Chapters Six and Seven survey past and current U.S. policies for dealing with poverty. Chapter Six highlights the ineffectiveness of U.S. policies in eliminating poverty by surveying a long history of misguided theories and stingy programs up through the late 1980s. Chapter Seven then picks up the story of the current wave of punitive welfare reforms into the late 1990s, explaining why these reforms cannot and will not reduce poverty, but will instead increase hardship.

In Chapters Eight and Nine, we offer our alternative policy vision—drawing on the insights and ideas of activists and advocates around the country. We propose positive reforms in welfare itself in Chapter Eight, and then in Chapter Nine, lay out a broader agenda for economic justice for women and low-income families. Finally, in Chapter Ten, we suggest the elements of a *political* strategy to make this policy vision a reality.

In writing this book, we have wrestled repeatedly with problems of terminology. When we started the book, Aid to Families with Dependent Children (AFDC), a cash aid program primarily assisting low-income single mothers and their children, existed as a single national program administered by the states. The federal welfare "reform" legislation of 1996, which we discuss in depth in Chapter Seven, replaced this program with fifty state programs, each partially funded by a federal block grant dubbed Temporary Assistance to Needy Families (TANF). The term "welfare" could be used to refer to both systems of cash assistance. In many people's minds, however, "welfare" also describes other cash assistance such as unemployment compensation and Supplemental Security Income (SSI), and noncash benefits such as Food Stamps and Medicaid. Moreover, consistent application of the term "welfare" would extend it to middle- and upper-class benefits such as the tax deduction for mortgage interest, as well as "corporate welfare" programs that provide tax breaks or government financial assistance to a wide range of businesses, including many of the nation's largest.

There is no fully satisfactory solution to this naming problem, but here are the conventions we follow: When statistics or other facts apply specifically to the old AFDC program, we naturally use the name "AFDC." When we make statements that bridge the old and new systems, we refer to "AFDC/TANF" or, more often, to "welfare." (The new system is still too recent to document alone statistically.) Despite the many possible meanings of the word "welfare," in this book we use it primarily to mean "the welfare programs that used to be AFDC."

Despite recent destructive shifts in U.S. anti-poverty policy, we still believe that insight, empathy, and the political will to seriously confront poverty can make a comeback. In fact, we feel sure that as the consequences of bad policy unfold, growing numbers of Americans will search for better analysis and policy —not just with respect to women's poverty, but also the closely connected issues of work and family. We hope that this book will aid in that search.

1

Women, Income, and Poverty: There's a Family Connection

The more things change . . .

Women's lives have changed dramatically over the last forty years. Women find themselves in jobs, educational institutions, and public offices they never would have dreamed of in the 1950s. New social freedoms and economic opportunities mean that a woman living without a man is no longer considered an oddity.

But other things haven't changed so much. The American economic and political system has yet to catch up to the social and cultural strides women have made. Women's earnings are considerably lower than men's, approximately 70 cents to every man's dollar. Women are still primarily responsible for providing or finding child care and taking care of domestic chores. Thus, most women's economic fortunes still depend far too much on men's fortunes.

After four decades of economic, political, and social changes, women are by no means equal partners with men in economic or family life. Women, especially those with children, who have moved up the corporate ladder hit the "glass ceiling"—that invisible barrier to further advancement—and are shunted off to the "mommy track." Many more women—particularly single mothers—with limited skills or support are stuck in a "bottomless pit" of poverty. While these two groups of women may seem a world apart, they have much in common—their economic opportunities are restricted because of their gender.

Aside from the few born to wealth, people in this country get their income from three main sources: sharing the income of other family members, earning income themselves in the labor market, and receiving income from the government. Earnings occupy the central place among the three, since they far exceed government-provided income and constitute the main source of income to be shared within families. But discrimination and job segregation limit women's access to labor market earnings. Child care demands additionally constrain many women's possibilities for paid work.

This inequity is particularly disastrous for single women with children. Half of all single mothers in the United States have incomes below the poverty line. Single mothers face the same obstacles as other women *plus* the lack of a spouse's income—leaving many of them dependent on government-provided income.

As inflation eats away at cash benefits, and as state and federal legislators impose stringent requirements designed to thin the welfare rolls, poverty looks more and more like a bottomless pit. Sensible welfare reform, based on understanding the actual needs and capabilities of mothers, can give women a leg up out of poverty. But before we tackle the issues of poverty and welfare reform, it is important to place women's economic situation in a larger context. A good starting place is a brief look at four major economic trends affecting women, and many men as well.

A different world than our mothers faced: Four trends

Trend 1: The declining marriage rate

For a variety of reasons, marriage is not for everyone. Fewer and fewer women are getting or staying married (see Figure 1.1). As of 1995, close to 45 percent of women were *not* currently married.[1] (Annual Census Bureau surveys, unfortunately, do not make it possible to tell how many of these live with partners). Not staying married is an important part of this picture: about two-thirds of all first marriages (and an even higher proportion of remarriages) end in separation or divorce.[2]

Figure 1.1   More Women Are Not Married

Percentage of adult women who are unmarried, 1960–1995

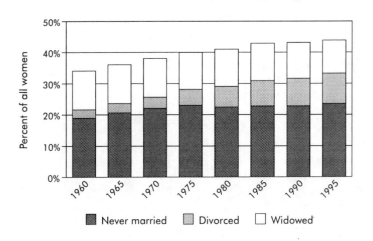

Source: U.S. Bureau of the Census, *Household and Family Characteristics*, various years.

But just because fewer women are married doesn't mean they aren't raising children. One-half of all females over sixteen have custody of a child under the age of eighteen. And of those women with children, one out of every three is not married. This means that *one woman out of six is a single mother*.

Trend 2: The growing labor market

Work, both unpaid and paid, can be an important way to interact with the world and a source of pride. Increasingly, women are doing *both* kinds of work—unpaid work in the home and work for pay outside the home. More and more women—and especially more and more mothers—are in the paid labor force (see Figure 1.2). Two out of every three mothers also have a paid job outside the home.

In 1947, a woman was only 38 percent as likely to be working or looking for work as a man. By 1996, that percentage had more than doubled to 79 percent. Of course, these patterns differed by race: for example, black women have always been more likely to work than white or Latina women. But the overall trend pre-

Figure 1.2 More Women and Fewer Men Are in the Paid Labor Force *Labor force participation rates* of men and women sixteen years of age and older, 1955–1995*

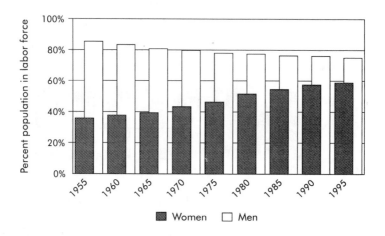

*The labor force participation rate is equal to the numbers of those employed plus those looking for work divided by the adult population. That number is multiplied by 100 to get a percentage.
Source: *Economic Report of the President, 1996.*

vails across racial boundaries. Black women were 54 percent as likely to be in the paid labor force as black men in 1954, and 88 percent as likely in 1996.

More work for women has not translated into equal pay. Women usually don't work as many hours a week outside the home as men do, and for every hour they do work, women earn less than men. Nationwide in 1955, a woman working full-time, year-round earned 64 percent as much as her male counterpart. Women actually fell further behind during the 1960s and 1970s, and then gained some ground in the 1980s and 1990s, leaving them with 71 percent of male earnings in 1995—only slightly better than in 1955 (see Figure 1.3).

Although women make two-thirds of what men do for every hour they work, because women work fewer hours a year than men do—mostly because of family-care responsibilities—women's average *annual* earnings stand at one-half those of

Figure 1.3 Women's Earnings Still Lag Behind Men's

Median earnings* of year-round, full-time male and female workers in 1995 dollars in the United States, 1955–1995

□ Women's earnings   ■ Men's earnings   ●— Female-male ratio

*Median earnings is the earnings level where 50% earn more and 50% earn less than that amount.

Source: U.S. Bureau of the Census, *Current Population Reports*, series P60, various years.

men, even among those who are heads and spouses. Among all heads and spouses employed, men averaged $28,690 per year in 1993; women averaged only $14,120 a year.[3]

Trend 3: The decline of manufacturing work

While more women are in the labor force and more jobs are open to women today than they were thirty years ago, other changes in the structure of the economy have also had important impacts on men and women. One of those changes is the steady decline of manufacturing jobs—especially high-paying jobs in heavy industries such as auto, steel, and aircraft—and the corresponding steady increase in the percentage of service jobs. The phenomenon, popularly referred to as the "deindustrialization" of America, is easy to see in Figure 1.4.[4] In 1955, one-third of all jobs were in manufacturing; by 1995, the figure had fallen to one-sixth. Conversely, in 1955, the service and retail industries

Figure 1.4 More Service and Fewer Manufacturing Jobs in the Economy. *Percentage of persons employed in manufacturing and in service and retail industry jobs, 1955–1995*

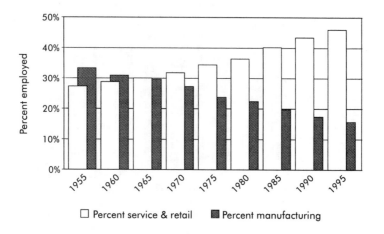

Source: *Economic Report of the President,* table B-42, 1996.

accounted for about one-quarter of all jobs; by 1995, they represented almost one-half. And while not all jobs in the manufacturing sector pay high wages, and not all jobs in the service sector pay low wages, there is a strong correlation between pay and industry sector. In 1995, the average weekly paycheck from a manufacturing job was $514, 85 percent higher than the average pay in the service and retail industries.[5]

Those particularly hurt by the decline in manufacturing jobs are younger workers without a college education. Also, since men have historically held the vast majority of manufacturing jobs, deindustrialization has had a profoundly negative effect on their earnings, which can be seen in Figure 1.3. Although women are concentrated in the growing service sector, deindustrialization has not helped women's wages either—with the possible exception of women with higher levels of education.

While the reasons for the change in the structure of the economy are complex, rapid technological changes, increased international competition, and concerted corporate strategies to

Figure 1.5   The Feminization of Poverty

Poor persons in female-headed families as a percentage of all poor persons, 1960–1995

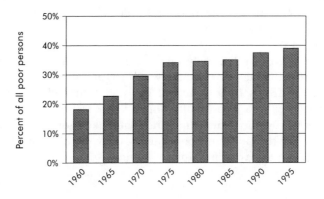

Source: U.S. Bureau of the Census, *Poverty in the United States: 1995*, P60–194, 1996.

maximize profits all play important roles. The impact on families has been clear. Men's earning power has declined—especially that of men who are not in high levels of management. The days when the majority of middle-class men could support an entire family on their paychecks are pretty much gone. Middle-class women's entry into the labor force is partly due to increased desires to have more economic independence and partly due to financial necessity.

Trend 4: The poverty trap

With the marriage rate declining and men's incomes falling, more and more women rely less and less on men's income for support. Unfortunately, the labor market has taken up only some of the income slack. Therefore, it is not surprising to find more women and their families slipping into poverty. Even though women are now more likely to work for pay, many do not earn enough to support themselves and a family. For the growing number of families headed by women only, the end result is financial disaster. In 1995, almost two out of every five people who were poor lived in families consisting of a single woman plus dependents. This is more than twice the rate in 1960 (see Figure 1.5).

In 1993, 16 percent of all families and lone individuals were poor. At the same time, 52 percent of single-mother families—or *one out of every two*—were poor. Compare this to an 11 percent (or one out of every ten) poverty rate for two-adult families with children.

Poverty is most definitely a women's issue, and it has been for a long time. Of all poor adults, two-thirds are women. Poverty is also a children's issue: one out of every four children in this country lives in a poor family—most likely a family with only a woman to support him or her. And that makes government policies toward the poor and poor families a women's issue, as certainly as equal pay or freedom of choice.

Pretzel logic:
Contradictory values about work and family

Four contradictions cloud political thinking about women, families, and poverty.

Contradiction 1: Family values vs. valuing families

In the early 1990s, when Vice President Dan Quayle attacked television character Murphy Brown (portrayed by Candice Bergen) for choosing to have a child without a husband, the resulting political flap energized a discussion over what constitutes family values. That discussion continues today. In a display of uncommon unity, most people agree on the importance of care and concern for family and community, hard work, commitment, and instilling moral and spiritual values in children. But fewer agree on what a *family is* or *should be*. Further, the debate highlights an important contradiction in the thinking of most Americans:

- *On the one hand*, we are a country that says we should value families and, above all else, children. After all, everyone agrees that children are the future of our country. *On the other hand*, we are a country that doesn't value the *work* of taking care of children.

In the United States, childcare is every individual family's responsibility. Typically, the burden falls on women. Mothers take care of children for free, while childcare workers are paid embarrassingly low wages.

Contradiction 2: The obligation to work vs. the opportunity to work

The nationwide recession in the early 1990s showed that almost all of us are potentially vulnerable to economic downturns. The lackluster recovery and rampant corporate downsizing painfully demonstrate that even in the midst of historic profit levels and what appear to be positive economic indicators, for most employees job security is by no means assured. The icy hand of unemployment has even touched people who thought they had a job for life—middle managers and midcareer professionals at large companies like IBM and AT&T. These experiences serve as a chilly reminder of the second contradiction:

- *On the one hand*, we believe that able-bodied adults have an obligation to work. Many sing the praises of the hardworking people in the working and middle classes, implicitly or explicitly scorning the idle rich and—especially—the shiftless poor. Horatio Alger's vision of upward mobility through diligence, resourcefulness, and thrift still dominates. *On the other hand,* as a nation, we make no commitment to ensure that jobs are there for those willing and able to work. Indeed, the federal government has backed further and further away from any commitments to pursue full employment, and the average unemployment rate has climbed decade by decade.

Without available jobs, the principle of an obligation to work rings hollow.

Contradiction 3: Having a job vs. having a living wage

The number of people who work yet are still poor is at its highest in decades. In 1995, 10 percent of adult workers below the poverty line (and a full 12 percent of poor adults under age sixty-five) actually held a *year-round, full-time* job (see Figure 1.6).[6] The growth in low-wage jobs and the erosion of the minimum wage in inflation-adjusted dollars means that many employed

Figure 1.6   Working But Poor

Percentage of poor adults who worked year-round, full-time, 1966–1995

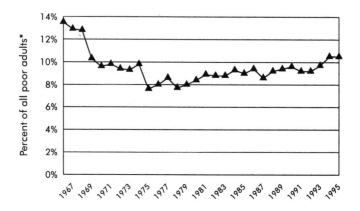

*Between 1966 and 1978, includes persons fourteen years of age and older. Between 1979 and 1989, includes persons fifteen years of age and older. From 1990 onward, includes persons sixteen years of age and older.

Source: For 1966–1994, Center on Budget and Policy Priorities, *Poverty and Income Trends*, 1994 (using *Current Population Reports*), p. 77. For 1995, U.S. Bureau of the Census, *Poverty in the United States: 1995*, P60-194, p. 17.

people don't earn enough to buy the basic necessities for themselves or their families. This highlights a contradiction that many thought this country had eradicated thirty years ago:

- *On the one hand*, we believe that a job is the best way out of poverty. Those with the opportunity to hold a job can and should be self-sufficient. Able-bodied adults are expected to take care of themselves because hard work pays off in the labor market. *On the other hand*, as a nation, we give no assurance that people with jobs will earn enough to support themselves, nor any guarantee of health insurance or even steady work.

Without jobs that pay living wages, the current emphasis on work as a ticket out of poverty is a cruel joke.

Contradiction 4: Legitimate vs. illegitimate dependencies
The commonly held notion of the "undeserving poor" points to yet another contradiction:

- *On the one hand*, dependency within the family is considered natural. When a breadwinner provides for his or her family, we don't question the moral fiber of those dependent on the primary wage earner. Indeed, when one spouse stays home to cook, clean, and care for the children, this represents *inter*-dependence—a division of labor. *On the other hand*, many denounce dependency on the government as pitiable at best, reprehensible at worst. A woman who stays home to cook, clean, and care for her children *without* a husband is often viewed as taking unfair advantage of government generosity. But why not recognize this as another kind of *inter*dependence at the level of the community or the whole society?

As these four contradictions play themselves out, women—especially women with children and women of color—and increasing numbers of men are feeling the squeeze.

Scapegoating poor women and their children

Politicians and pundits have targeted social safety net programs, particularly welfare programs directed toward single mothers and their children, as wasteful and even as the *cause* of poverty in this country.[7] They have scapegoated poor women and their children. By playing on people's economic insecurity, these policymakers have avoided addressing the contradictions just outlined—promoting instead state and national surges to decimate the programs that support poor families. This is not only a morally repugnant strategy, it is also economically bankrupt. It avoids dealing with the most basic economic issues facing women today and will result in more poverty, not less.

There are many things wrong with the welfare system, but it has always served as an absolutely vital lifeline for many families. And some form of public assistance for women raising children alone has always been necessary in an economy that makes wage-earning the most important source of income.

In this book, we offer an alternative way to look at and under-stand women's economic situation—from the bottom up. Many of the problems facing the poorest of women in this country are not all that different from those facing the richest. And increas-ingly, as men begin to take on more family responsibility and face dimmer economic opportunities than in the past, they too are being held back, not by welfare mothers, but by an economic system built on contradictions that place family and work de-mands in competition with one another.

The bottom of the bottomless pit

Government programs to provide income to poor single moth-ers and their children affect *all* women because, in three impor-tant ways, these welfare laws define the floor of how low women can sink in this economy.

First, and most immediately, the level of welfare payments and the regulations on welfare receipt make up the "safety net" for any woman with a child. Half of the single mothers in this coun-try are poor, but only about one-third of all single mothers re-ceived Aid to Families with Dependent Children (AFDC) before that program was abolished, and fewer still will be eligible to receive money from its replacement, Temporary Assistance to Needy Families (TANF). If, as a woman, you find yourself sup-porting a family on your own—for whatever reason—you have a one in three chance of having to rely on welfare. What are your chances of ending up in this situation? Currently, one woman in six is a single mother. And many middle-class women are only a divorce, a layoff notice, or a pregnancy away from poverty. The existence of a wide safety net is essential for women's economic security.

Second, each time welfare benefits are slashed, eligibility rules are tightened, or workfare requirements are added, more women in need of jobs and income flood the workforce. While most welfare recipients have limited education and skills, and consequently compete at the low end of the labor market, this competition has a ripple effect that reaches up to higher-skill jobs. At each level of the labor market, workers feel competitive pressure from those just a little below. Like the minimum wage or restrictions on child labor, decent welfare provisions not only protect recipients themselves, but shield other workers from rock-bottom competition.

Third, a bit more abstract but perhaps even more important, welfare policies indicate how the political and economic system regards women's work—all women's work, not just that of poor women. AFDC/TANF is designed to provide the income supplements that mothers need when they lack male income. Across the forty-eight contiguous states, the median welfare payment for a family of three is 38 percent of the poverty line—and almost sure to fall farther. In 1996, the maximum AFDC benefit for a family of three in the most generous state—New York—was $703 a month, while the least generous state—Mississippi—paid a meager $120.[8] The poverty line for a family of three in 1996 was $12,980 (that's $1,082 a month). Even adding in the cash value of Food Stamps, welfare leaves families below the poverty level. In 1996, the value of AFDC and Food Stamps combined for a family of three was $935 in New York and $433 in Mississippi. In the median state, the combined package was worth only 65 percent of the poverty line. By keeping payments so low, our political system ratifies an economic system that pays women far less than men and does not value (in terms of anything other than rhetoric) the work of caring for families.

Women are poor for a reason

Half of all single-mother families in this country are poor—but not because they are lazy, lack initiative, or are unlucky. The primary reason is because it is difficult for one adult to support a family, and even harder if that adult is female. Mothers must do unpaid work, limiting their time to do paid work, and when they do paid work, they are paid significantly less than men.

Childcare responsibilities affect women at all income levels. As women with children know, it is very hard to work full-time and care for children as well. Part-time jobs rarely pay enough for one person to live on, let alone an entire family. Most of the good full-time jobs that pay enough to support an entire family assume there's a "wife" at home, and accordingly, make large demands on the worker's time and flexibility. Highly paid women who choose to be mothers (and cannot simply turn their lives over to the company) face the second-class status of being on the horizontal "mommy track" rather than the vertical job ladder many male or childless women workers climb to higher pay and prestige.

Finding childcare is a problem for any family. And all women face the reality of lower pay than men. But for single mothers, these issues collide in a devastating combination. Welfare policies that inadequately address these issues implicitly and explicitly deny and devalue what women contribute to their families, workplaces, and communities in the form of unpaid labor.

Better policies

Two dead-end theories dominate debates about welfare reform. First, politicians argue that single mothers must be made to work in the paid labor market. But, as politicians know full well, most single mothers already work as much as they can. Further, as surveys indicate, many mothers receiving welfare would like to work. The real issue, then, is not whether or not to work, but whether paid work is available, how much it pays, and how to balance work and childcare.

Second, many policymakers encourage replacing the social responsibilities of government assistance with individual family responsibilities: make men pay child support, require welfare recipients to change their behavior, or even pressure single women to find a man. While child support can help, for most single mothers it offers a poor substitute for reliable government assistance. Penalizing women and their children for ascribed behaviors (such as having more children to collect welfare) that are supported by anecdotes and not facts is mean-spirited at best. The ultimate examples of legislating family responsibility are the recent debates and policies that attempt to establish who has the right to have and raise children. Forced coupling or relegating poor families' children to orphanages are policies as unworkable as they are undesirable. Because such policies inevitably result in the legislation of women's behavior and morality, women have the most at stake in discussions about the "right" kind of families.

What should be done instead?

In a vacuum, welfare reform can only solve a small part of the problem. Breaking the connection between gender and poverty requires changing the world of work as well. So, if we as a nation are serious about reducing the poverty of women and children, we need to invest in eight kinds of institutional changes. We summarize these eight changes here and make a more detailed case for them in Chapter Nine.

1. Create an income-maintenance system that realizes the need for full-time childcare. Let's truly value families and acknowledge the reality of children's needs. That means financially supporting families engaged in full-time childcare and providing alternate sources of childcare for those who work outside the home.

2. Create jobs that don't assume you have a "wife" at home to perform limitless unpaid work. Create the opportunity to work, for poor women and poor men as well. Full employment is an old idea that still makes sense. And it's not just the welfare system that has to come to terms with family needs; it's employers, too. With women making up 46 percent of the workforce—and men taking on more childcare responsibilities—a change in work styles is overdue.

3. Close the gender gap in pay, and boost wages to a living level. One way to achieve gender pay equity is to require employers to reevaluate the ways in which they compensate comparable skills. Poor women need pay equity most, but all women need it. Another way to close the pay gap is to increase the minimum wage. Most minimum-wage workers are women. An increase from the current $5.15 an hour to $5.91 would bring the minimum wage to 50 percent of the average wage—the original target for minimum-wage legislation. Yet another wage booster would be to support unionization and end the unfair advantages of anti-union employers. Unions raise pay levels most for the lowest paid. Also, we need stronger affirmative action to continue breaking down job segregation by race and gender.

4. Tame the family budget busters—housing and health care. If leaving welfare and taking a job means giving up health benefits and housing subsidies, it's awfully hard to make the transition. Although high-salary workers receive health benefits and can readily afford housing, low-wage workers don't have these advantages. Government should provide these supports; universal health care is an important first step.

5. *Expand the safety net.* Extending unemployment insurance and temporary disability insurance (which five states have already done) could help pick up some of the slack and encourage parents to combine work and childcare.

6. *Make education and training affordable and available for all.* In an economy where the premium on skills and education is increasing, education and training are necessities for young people *and* adults, women *and* men.

7. *Promote community-based economic development.* Low- and moderate-income communities across the country are tapping their own underutilized resources to build housing, create jobs, and provide services. They deserve financial and technical support.

8. *Secure funding with a fair tax structure.* Many of these proposals require government spending that is consistent with the ways in which our counterparts in other industrialized countries spend money—especially for universal child allowances, education and training, and universal health care coverage. The United States needs to seriously consider how much and whom it taxes. Taxes paid by the wealthiest families as a percentage of their income have fallen dramatically over the last fifteen years, while the burden on the bottom 80 percent of us has risen. Federal, state, and local governments have taxed middle- and low-income families for too long without assuring them of the basic benefits they increasingly can't afford. A strong case can be made for universal social programs funded by a fair tax system based on the ability to pay. The alternative—not funding child allowances, health care, and training—may prove more costly to society in the long run.

Notes

1. U.S. Bureau of the Census, *Marital Status and Living Arrangements: March 1994*, P20-484, table 1 (1996).
2. Teresa Castro Martin and Larry L. Bumpass, "Recent Trends in Marital Disruption," *Demography*, vol. 26, no. 1 (1989): 37-51.

3. Calculated by authors from the March 1994 Current Population Survey. (The Current Population Survey is a monthly survey of a sample of U.S. households, conducted by the U.S. Bureau of the Census. Every March the Census Bureau asks households more detailed questions about their income in the previous year.) A primary earner is either the head of a household or the spouse of the head.

4. This term was made popular by Barry Bluestone and Bennett Harrison in their book *The Deindustrialization of America* (New York: Basic Books, 1982).

5. Calculated by authors from U.S. Bureau of Labor Statistics, *Employment and Earnings* (January 1996), tables B-1 and B-2. Much of the weekly pay difference results from the fact that service and retail workers are more likely to work part-time. The hourly manufacturing wage, however, is still 29 percent above the hourly wage in service and retail.

6. U.S. Bureau of the Census, *Poverty in the United States: 1995*, P60-194 (Washington, D.C.: Government Printing Office, 1996), table 3, p. 17.

7. For profiles of two of the most prominent purveyors of this view, see the discussion of Charles Murray of the American Enterprise Institute and Robert Rector of the Heritage Foundation, in Chapter Six.

8. Benefits in New York apply only to Suffolk County. Alaska and Hawaii have higher benefits, but also have higher poverty income thresholds. Data were prepared by the Congressional Research Service on the basis of a telephone survey.

2

Who's Poor?
Patterns of Poverty

Who's responsible?

The United States—far more than other countries—worships the "individual." People admire and promote the ability of individuals to rise above adversity and take control of their environment through self-initiative. Stories of the "self-made man" abound, and a whole folklore glorifies the "rugged individual," underscoring the notion that people's fortunes (or misfortunes) are largely of their own making.

While it is clear that individuals need to take responsibility for themselves, there are two problems with blaming those who don't seem to be pulling themselves up by their own bootstraps. First, the playing field is not level. Deeply embedded attitudes about race, gender, and class color our economic and social institutions and limit access and opportunity, keeping many from succeeding despite their perseverance. With an officially acceptable 6 percent level of unemployment (the rate the Federal Reserve Bank argues is consistent with low levels of inflation) and a minimum wage far below its level of twenty or thirty years ago (after adjusting for inflation), "losers" are built-in—almost inevitable—in our economic system. Second, no one is truly self-made. We all grow up in families, and we all need the support and care of communities. Behind every successful person is a network of people who have provided him or her with much of the necessary confidence, care, family resources, and inspiration. And *lack* of economic success often has more to do with shortcomings in these areas than with any lack of gumption.

This chapter places individual wealth and poverty in a family context, examining who is most likely to be poor in the United States.

Who's poor and how do you know? Measuring poverty in the United States

This chapter is chock-full of official U.S. poverty statistics. But who decides who is poor, and how do they know?

The Census Bureau of the Department of Commerce officially collects and publishes poverty data in the United States. The origins of these poverty statistics lie in the early 1960s, when Mollie Orshansky, a staff economist for the Social Security Administration, developed the concept of a poverty threshold for different types of families that was adopted by the Office of Economic Opportunity (OEO) in 1965. The OEO, as the main agency in charge of carrying out the Johnson administration's "War on Poverty," needed a concrete and consistent measure of poverty to know if it was winning the war.[1]

The poverty rates used here (and by the Census Bureau) are based on an absolute measure of poverty. That is, they are based on a set dollar amount—a threshold income. If you live in a family that has an annual income below that threshold, you are officially counted as poor by the Census Bureau. The OEO chose to use an absolute definition of poverty—rather than a relative one, which would measure how much worse off the poor are than everybody else—because they thought they had a better chance of eliminating poverty if measured in this way. In 1996, the official annual income poverty threshold for a family of four consisting of two adults and two children was $15,600.

Where do the threshold incomes come from? From Mollie Orshansky. In the early 1960s, based on consumer household expenditure data from the 1950s, she determined the cost of a minimum adequate diet for different family types. At the time of the surveys, food accounted for about one-third of low-income families' total budget, so she multiplied the different food budgets by three to arrive at the poverty income thresholds. Those thresholds, indexed for inflation, are still used today. So the present poverty threshold for a family of four is merely the 1963 poverty threshold income for that family type ($3,100) adjusted for changes in consumer prices.

Because different families consume different amounts of food, the poverty income thresholds vary based on family size and composition. Families with persons aged sixty-five and older have lower poverty income thresholds than families of the same size without older members. And due to economies of scale, the poverty income threshold for a family of four is much less than double that of a family of two.

The way in which poverty is measured is of far more importance than just research. As economist James Tobin remarked in the late 1960s, "Adoption of a specific quantitative measure, no matter how arbitrary and debatable, will have durable and far-reaching consequences. Administrations will be judged by their success or failure at reducing the officially measured prevalence of poverty."[2] In addition, the poverty line's definition matters in a very practical way, since so many government programs base eligibility on the poverty level. Twenty-seven of the seventy federal and federal-state programs that provide either cash or in-kind aid to low-income persons are directly linked to established official poverty guidelines.

The advantages of the current measurement of poverty are that it remains consistent over time, it adjusts for need, and, at least initially, it was based on some real measure of adequate income level for basic survival. Still, many argue that the measure is deeply flawed and underestimates poverty. Probably the biggest problem with the U.S. poverty income thresholds is that they have not been adjusted for changes in consumption patterns since they were established. Today, food represents less than one-third of total family expenditures—housing, childcare, and medical costs have become larger components of people's budgets. Orshansky herself has said that the poverty measure should be periodically adjusted to reflect expenditure changes.

There's another problem with the measure: it is based on surveys that ask about annual income, which probably underestimates the extent of poverty. Many families are poor for several months out of the year, even though their total annual income may be above the poverty line. These families are not counted among the poor. For example, Urban Institute researchers found that while the annual poverty rate was 14.4 percent in 1984, the percentage of persons who were poor for at least one month during that year was 26.2 percent.

Still another problem with the current measure is that it does not account for wide variations in the cost of living across states and regions, and sometime even within states. Most notably, heating and housing costs are dramatically higher in the Northeast than they are in the South. Using one standard income threshold for all families, regardless of where they live, does not really project a consistent measure.

Some argue instead that the present measure *over*estimates poverty. In the 1980s, conservatives in the Reagan administration attacked the poverty threshold as being too high, claiming that the annual adjustment index overestimated inflation. In its place, they established an alternative index that estimated a lower rate of inflation, and as a result, lowered the poverty income threshold. With the mere stroke of a pen, the Reagan administration reduced the poverty rate!

Others argue that in estimating poverty, noncash income, like Food Stamps, should be included as income. Poverty rates would then be lower for those who receive such benefits. This is absolutely true, but poverty calculations also do not exempt income that goes toward taxes, health care costs, or costs of working, such as transportation or childcare. Payroll taxes, state sales taxes, and local property taxes take a large percentage of low-income people's budgets. If after-tax income (including Food Stamps) were measured and then adjusted for costs, the poverty rate would be considerably higher.

In a recent report, a panel of poverty experts assembled by the Committee on National Statistics at the National Research Council published their findings on measuring poverty in the United States.[3] They found the current measurement inadequate for all the reasons mentioned above, and they recommended a new measure that takes into account in-kind benefits (like Food Stamps and housing subsidies) and out-of-pocket expenses (like taxes and childcare), and is based on recently collected data on the costs of food, clothing, and housing (adjusted for differences among geographic areas). Even using a low estimate of the income level necessary to fulfill a family's basic needs, the panel found that once income is adjusted for in-kind benefits and certain costs, poverty rates in the United States are currently being underestimated. Using 1992 data, the panel estimated that the poverty rate for all persons would have been 18.1 percent using their proposed measure, instead of the official 14.5 percent.

There are ways of measuring poverty other than an absolute income threshold. In several multicountry studies of poverty in the 1980s and 1990s, a group of poverty researchers defined the poverty threshold for each country as 50 percent of its median income. We discuss findings from these studies in Chapter Six. Using this measure, U.S. poverty rates were considerably higher than those calculated by the U.S. Census Bureau. The benefit of this alternate measure is that it makes poverty a *relative* concept—measuring how a nation's poorest compare with those in the middle. This also makes comparisons across countries much easier. A disadvantage is that the direction of change in poverty rates can be deceptive. For example, poverty rates could easily fall in a recession if the median income falls faster than the income of people at the very bottom of the income scale.

In short, the definition of poverty is a subjective choice on the part of policymakers and researchers, only loosely based on a measure of an income that meets basic family needs.

Women, children, and people of color first

Despite the problems with the current measure, this book reports the "official" poverty rates as defined by the Census Bureau. Any way you slice the data, however, the poor are disproportionately comprised of people of color, children, and women. While only one out of six Americans is nonwhite, people of color represent one-third of the poor. Only 27 percent of the U.S. population is under eighteen, yet children comprise 40 percent of all poor people. Similarly, women account for 51 percent of all people aged eighteen and over, but make up 62 percent of those adults who live in poverty.

For close to 100 years, social scientists have documented the extremely uneven distribution of poverty. In recent decades, many conducting research in this vein have noted that the most common face of poverty in the United States among adults is a woman's. Sociologist Diana Pearce dubbed this phenomenon the "feminization of poverty." Economist Nancy Folbre added that the highest risk of poverty comes from being female *and* having children—which helps explain the high rates of both female and child poverty in the United States. Folbre called this trend the "pauperization of motherhood."[4]

The financial disadvantages of being female—and especially of being a mother—are clear and consistent. Figures 2.1 to 2.6 and the data in Tables 2.1 and 2.2 all show that no matter how you look at the population, women are more likely than men to be poor. But it's not just gender that matters. Race, ethnicity, education, age, and family type all greatly affect the probability of being poor as well.

Let's start with race and ethnicity (depicted in Figure 2.1). Compared to whites, African Americans and Latinos are three times as likely to be poor, Native Americans are more than twice as likely to be poor, and Asians' odds of poverty are one and a half times as great. Black and Latina women fare the worst, with poverty rates around 30 percent.

City dwellers are more often poor than suburbanites or residents of rural areas—or, to put it another way, poor people are most likely to live in the city (see Figure 2.2). Almost one in

Table 2.1 Who's Poor

Percentage of people who are poor, by selected characteristics, 1993

	All	Men	Women	Children
All	15.1%	9.7%	14.9%	22.6%
By race/ethnicity				
White	9.9	6.8	10.5	13.5
Black	32.9	19.8	31.5	45.7
Latino	30.6	20.6	29.3	40.9
Asian	15.2	12.8	15.3	18.0
Native American	23.4	15.8	23.1	32.3
By residence				
Central city	22.3	13.8	21.0	35.1
Suburb, small city	10.1	6.7	9.9	14.8
Rural	17.3	11.5	17.7	24.4

Source: Calculated by authors from U.S. Bureau of the Census, Current Population Survey, 1994.

Figure 2.1   U.S. Poverty Rates by Race and Ethnicity, 1993

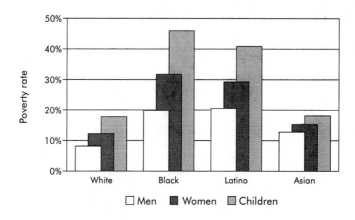

Note: Latinos may be of any race.
Source: Calculated by authors from U.S. Bureau of the Census, Current Population Survey, March 1994.

Figure 2.2   U.S. Poverty Rates by Residence, 1993

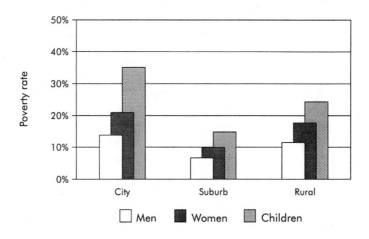

Source: Calculated by authors from U.S. Bureau of the Census, Current Population Survey, March 1994.

Table 2.2 Education Staves Off Poverty, but Women Need More of It to Keep Up with Men *Poverty rates for adults, 1993*

Years of education	Poverty rates		
	All adults	Men	Women
8 or less	30.2%	25.2%	35.1%
9–11	26.0	19.0	32.2
12	12.0	9.4	14.1
13–15	8.3	6.6	9.8
16	4.1	3.7	4.6
17+	2.9	2.7	3.1

Source: Calculated by authors from U.S. Bureau of the Census, Current Population Survey, 1994.

seven residents of what the Census Bureau calls "central cities" (the 100 or so largest hub cities, such as New York, Cleveland, Houston, or San Francisco) is poor, compared to one in fifteen residents in smaller cities and suburbs. Poverty rates in rural areas fall between these two groups.

Education helps lift people out of poverty; conversely, the poor are less likely to finish high school or gain access to higher education (Figure 2.3 and Table 2.2). The poverty rate among high school dropouts is nearly two and a half times that of high school graduates and six times that of four-year-college graduates. For women, education is particularly important in staving off poverty. Four years of college sharply reduce their chances of being poor: from 14 percent to under 5 percent. But the gender gap persists: women with a high school diploma face poverty one and a half times more than male high school graduates.

Among women, both the youngest and the oldest are more commonly poor than those in between. But, as Figure 2.4 reveals, this "U" pattern does not hold for men. Among men, the poverty rate varies far less and shows no upturn among the elderly.

Another pattern that applies most strongly for women is the connection between having children and poverty—the pauperization of motherhood. For women, having at least one child under eighteen increases the chance of being poor from 12 percent

Figure 2.3   U.S. Poverty Rates by Years of Education, 1993

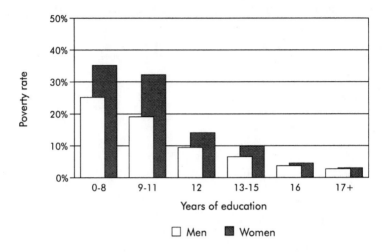

Source: Calculated by authors from U.S. Bureau of the Census, Current Population Survey, March 1994.

Figure 2.4   U.S. Poverty Rates by Age, 1993

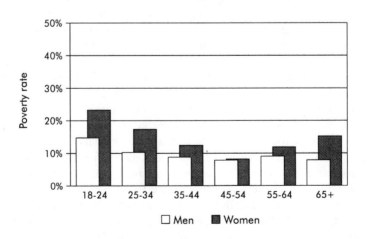

Source: Calculated by authors from U.S. Bureau of the Census, Current Population Survey, March 1994.

Table 2.3   Disproportionate Poverty

Various groups as percent of population and percent of poor, 1993

	Percent of population	*Percent of poor*
By age		
0–17	26.7%	40.0%
18–64	61.4	50.5
65+	11.9	9.6
By race/ethnicity		
White	73.6	48.1
Black	12.5	27.1
Latino	10.2	20.7
Asian	2.8	2.9
Native American	0.6	0.9
By residence		
Central city	29.4	42.3
Suburb, small city	45.3	29.5
Rural	25.3	28.2

Source: Calculated by authors from U.S. Bureau of the Census, Current Population Survey, 1994.

to 19 percent; having a child under six boosts that probability up to 23 percent (Figure 2.5). For women, then, there is quite an economic penalty for raising a family! For men, on the other hand, the penalty is much smaller—though still present.

Figure 2.6 zeroes in on single mothers. Single mothers are more than four times as likely to be poor as other women. Women who are not single mothers fall into poverty at a rate only slightly higher than that of men. The poverty problem for women is, above all, a problem suffered by single mothers.

This quick tour through the poverty statistics has revealed disproportionate poverty over and over again. Tables 2.3 and 2.4 illustrate this directly. As Table 2.3 dramatizes, children under eighteen are heavily overrepresented among the poor. Non-Latino whites, almost three-quarters of the U.S. population, account for less than half of the poor, though they are still the largest group of poor people. African Americans, Latinos, and Native Americans make up proportions of the poor population that are double their proportions of the overall population. De-

Figure 2.5   U.S. Poverty Rates by Presence and Age of Children, 1993

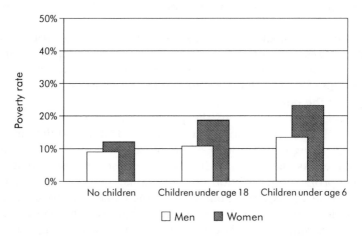

Source: Calculated by authors from U.S. Bureau of the Census, Current Population Survey, March 1994.

Figure 2.6   The Pauperization of Motherhood

Poverty rates for single mothers, other women, and men, 1993

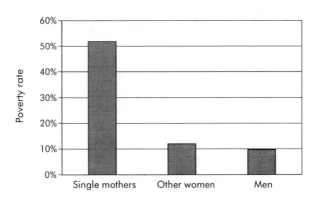

Note: Poverty rates are only for single mothers who do not live with any adult family members.

Source: Calculated by authors from U.S. Bureau of the Census, Current Population Survey, March 1994.

spite these disproportional odds, it is important to point out that—counter to stereotypes—the typical poor person is white, and that blacks make up only one-quarter of the poor population.

Nearly one-half of Americans live in the suburbs (surrounding the central cities of metropolitan areas), but less than one-third of poor Americans do. For central-city residents, the reverse is true: they are less than one-third of the population, but close to half of the poor.

Finally, let's return to the predicament of single mothers. Though they account for a slim 4 percent of all U.S. adults, single moms living without other adults represent over 15 percent of poor adults (Table 2.4). Other women constitute a slightly less-than-proportional fraction of poor adults. Men, who are about half of all adults, are the big winners: their share falls to just over one-third of poor adults. Again, it is important to notice that although single mothers are at much higher risk for falling below the poverty line than other adults, they still make up only a small fraction of all poor adults.

In short, the odds of ending up poor fall disproportionately on certain groups in the U.S. population. At the same time, many stereotypes of "the typical poor person" are misleading. African Americans, central-city dwellers, and single mothers each make up only a minority of poor people. A black single mother living in a central city is five times as likely as the average adult to be poor—but only one poor adult in sixteen is a black, central-city single mother.

Table 2.4   The Odds Are Against Single Mothers

Single mothers and other adults as percentage of all adults and percentage of poor adults, 1993

	Percent of all adults	Percent of poor adults
Single mothers	3.7%	15.5%
Other women	48.3	46.9
Men	48.0	37.7

Source: Calculated by authors from U.S. Bureau of the Census, Current Population Survey, 1994.

Poverty: A family problem

These numbers reveal the *patterns* of poverty, but they do not tell us the *causes*. Why are people poor? We start with a deceptively simple answer: people are poor because they lack resources—mostly, but not exclusively, income.

But this answer is not as simple as it appears. People gain access to resources in a variety ways. One obvious way is to go out and exchange what you have (usually the ability to perform work) in return for an income. Earnings—wages, salaries, and money gained from self-employment—are the main source 'of support for most families. But not all family members work. All of us have depended on someone else's income to support us for at least some part of our lives. When we are children, we must look to our parents for resources, and as we age, many turn to the government as a major source of support.

So, it is not just an individual's lack of resources that makes a person poor; it is their *family's* lack of resources. Poverty is a family (or household) concept—not an individual one. To get a clearer picture of women, work, poverty, and welfare, we need to take a closer look at families and the income they receive, the subject of the next chapter.

Notes

1. For a thorough discussion of the development of the U.S. poverty rate and alternative measures, see Patricia Ruggles, *Drawing the Line: Alternative Poverty Measures and Their Implications for Public Policy* (Washington, D.C.: Urban Institute, 1990).
2. Quoted in Ruggles, p. 4.
3. The committee's report was published by Constance F. Citro and Robert T. Michael, eds., *Measuring Poverty: A New Approach* (Washington, D.C.: National Academy Press, 1995).
4. Diana Pearce, "The Feminization of Poverty: Women, Work, and Welfare," *Urban and Social Change Review* (February 1978), and Nancy Folbre, "The Pauperization of Motherhood: Patriarchy and Social Policy in the U.S.," *Review of Radical Political Economics*, vol. 16, no. 4 (1985).

3

All in the Family: Family Types and Their Incomes

What does your family look like?

There are many types of families—single mothers, single fathers, gay and lesbian couples with and without children, related and unrelated people living in cooperative situations, "POSSLQs" (people of the opposite sex in the same living quarters), married and remarried couples with and without children, people who live alone, and even some "Ozzies and Harriets," the archetypal 1950s' family composed of breadwinner husband, homemaker wife, and two children. While married couples with children are still a large percentage of all families, these other family types are growing and are reshaping the cultural and social landscape. Schools, workplaces, churches and synagogues, and community and social groups are slowly coming to grips with the increasing diversity of family life. Government and business policies, however, have lagged in their responses.

While many researchers have recognized the important changes in family structures, it is not always easy to incorporate them into quantitative analysis. That's because the Census Bureau has been slow to recognize a more fluid definition of family. In its annual income survey, the Census Bureau defines families as people living in the same housing unit who are related by blood, marriage, or adoption. When using Census data, then, researchers who want to examine family income must make some rather arbitrary decisions about the "family" status of some household members. The difficulty comes when two or more unrelated individuals live in the same housing unit. Do you consider them unmarried partners, and hence pool their income for the best measure of family income? Or do you consider them roommates who share housing expenses but little else? While either assumption has problems, the information presented here takes the latter path, assuming that unrelated individuals do *not* share income.

In presenting these data, we encountered another ambiguity in how to view people who do not live with other family members. The Census Bureau refers to lone adults as "unrelated individuals" and typically presents data about these households separately from family data. But the family structure of any one individual often changes over time, and hence so does his or her access to income. Lone adults comprise a larger and larger percentage of the U.S. population, and more and more people find themselves in this situation at some point in their lifetime. To be as inclusive as possible and to present the full array of family types, we include lone adults as "families of one," although technically the Census Bureau does not consider such people to be families.

Yet another vexing question is how to identify the "head" of the family. For years, the U.S. Census Bureau automatically defined the husband, if present, as the head. Currently, the Census Bureau instead asks each family to identify the "householder" —the person in whose name the housing unit is owned or rented—and designates this person as the head. If there is no householder, or more than one, the Census Bureau allows the survey respondent to identify the head. We have followed this convention.

To talk about family income and potential access to income, we have chosen to categorize families by some of their most important income-generating characteristics: the number of adults, the presence of children, and the age and gender of the "head" (see Appendix A for a more detailed discussion of family types). Why does each of these factors matter?

Figure 3.1   All in the Family

Percentage of families of each type in the United States: 1973, 1979, 1987, and 1993

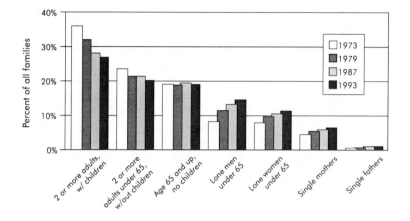

Source: Calculated by authors from U.S. Bureau of the Census, Current Population Survey, 1974, 1980, 1988, and 1994.

- The number of adults gives a first approximation of the number of people potentially available to perform work.
- When children are present, they decrease parents' ease of entering the paid workforce and typically increase the family's material needs without contributing to income.
- Earnings potential rises and then falls with age: people in their middle years (after schooling, but before old age and retirement) are likely to have the most time available for paid work and earn peak wages as well. On the other hand, savings —and the property income that entails—generally reach a maximum at the point of retirement.
- Among families with only one adult, gender matters because men still earn more than women.

Figure 3.1 shows the mix of family types over the last twenty years. The percentages of childless families with heads aged sixty-five and older as well as of married, childless couples have remained fairly constant at about 20 percent of the population each. The most rapidly *vanishing* family type is two or more adults (usually—but not necessarily—involving a married couple) with children under the age of eighteen. In 1973, this family type accounted for more than one out of every three families, but by 1993, after two decades of steady decline, the rate had shrunk to just over one in four. Further, of all families with children, two-adult families have seen their share fall from just under 87 percent in the early 1970s to 78 percent in 1993.

The most rapidly *growing* family type is lone men—those who do not live with any family members. Their relative numbers doubled between 1973 and 1993. The relative numbers of women living on their own (with or without children) also rose, from 8 percent in 1973 to 11 percent in 1993. And while the percentage of single-mother families has grown since 1973 from 5 percent to 7 percent, it remains a relatively small percentage of all family types.

Family structure, income, and poverty

Figure 3.2 depicts the poverty rates for those same families in 1993, and Table 3.1 compares each family type's share of all fami-

Figure 3.2   Poverty Rates for U.S. Families, 1993

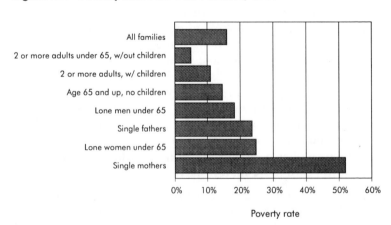

Source: Calculated by authors from U.S. Bureau of the Census, Current Population Survey, March1994.

Table 3.1 Disproportionate Poverty by Family Type

Family types as percentage of all families and percentage of poor families, 1993

Family type	Percent of all families	Percent of poor families
Two adults with children	26.9%	18.5%
Two adults without children (head under 65)	20.2	6.3
Single mother	6.6	21.4
Single father	1.2	1.7
Lone male (under 65)	14.7	16.9
Lone female (under 65)	11.4	17.8
Head over 65 (no children)	19.1	17.5

Source: Calculated by authors from U.S. Bureau of the Census, Current Population Survey, 1994.

lies with its share of families falling below the poverty line. Poverty rates vary considerably by family type (Figure 3.2): from 5 percent for families with at least two adults but no children to 52 percent for single-mother families. Family types' proportions of the poverty population (Table 3.1) tell the same story. Two-adult families with no children "trade places" with single mothers. Two-adult families without kids make up 20 percent of all families, but 6 percent of poor families, while single moms and their children represent 7 percent of all families, but 21 percent of poor families!

Family Money

These very disparate poverty rates suggest that different families have quite different access to income. One useful way to think about the difference is to look at each family type's income by source. We have lumped all income sources into four broad categories: pension and property income, earnings, government transfers, and interfamily transfers. Each variety of income is discussed below. Table 3.2 shows the percent of different family types that receive *any* income from each source, while Table 3.3 depicts the average annual amounts each family type received in 1993.

Table 3.2   Who's Getting Paid . . .

Percentage of families receiving any income from each major source, by family type, 1993

Family type	Pensions & property	Wages & salaries*	Government transfers	Interfamily transfers
All families	65%	78%	41%	6%
Two adults with children	67	97	28	8
Two adults without children (head under 65)	76	94	32	2
Single mother	32	69	49	35
Single father	42	91	26	7
Lone male (under 65)	50	87	20	7
Lone female (under 65)	56	82	22	7
Head over 65 (no children)	78	27	95	1

*Wages & salaries category includes self-employment income. Detailed definitions of income categories are provided in Appendix A.

Source: Calculated by authors from U.S. Bureau of the Census, Current Population Survey, 1994.

Property and pension income. One way people get income is by owning things—real estate and financial assets—that generate rent, dividends, interest, or royalties. People also receive income from their savings—in the form of either interest from current savings accounts or past savings paid out as a pension. While almost two out of every three families receive some of this type of income, only 10 percent get enough of it to lift their families out of poverty with property income alone—and over half of those are elder families. Most families have some income that comes from owning property or from past savings, but the potential for this type of income is highly circumscribed by one's age, earnings capability, and luck of birth. As Table 3.2 represents, families headed by someone over the age of sixty-five are most likely to have significant property and pension income. Two-adult families with no children have the second-largest average income from property and pension income. For single mothers the average amount of income from dividends, rent, interest, or pensions is $368, compared to $1,722 for two-adult families with children.

Table 3.3   . . . And How Much They're Getting Paid

Average annual family income* by income source, 1993

Family type	Pensions & property	Wages & salaries**	Gov't transfers	Interfamily transfers	Total***
Two adults with children	$1,722	$45,161 ·	$1,970	$294	$49,457
Two adults without children (head under 65)	4,768	45,043	2,546	129	52,816
Single mother	368	10,813	2,525	1,308	15,251
Single father	550	21,979	1,380	135	24,111
Lone male (under 65)	1,478	21,403	1,136	186	24,468
Lone female (under 65)	1,127	17,587	1,223	334	20,575
Head over 65 (no children)	8,404	5,565	10,547	34	24,674

*Average is for all families, including those with no income from a given category.

**Wages & salaries category includes self-employment income.

***Total includes "other" category. Detailed definitions of income categories are provided in Appendix A.

Source: Calculated by authors from U.S. Bureau of the Census, Current Population Survey, 1994.

Earnings. Most people work for a living. Work, in this case, means performing some service in exchange for cash, usually a paycheck from someone else. (About 10 percent of families have income from self-employment.) Almost four families out of five reported earnings in 1993, with those earnings supplying four out of every five dollars of income. But men and women score quite differently in dollars earned. In 1993, average earnings for women who worked were $16,771, compared to $27,475 for men. This reflects fewer hours worked by women over the year *and* women's lower hourly wages. How the gender wage gap affects a woman's economic well-being largely depends on whether other working-age adults—specifically men—are in her family.

Government transfers. Government assistance offers another source of income. Federal and state governments provide a wide variety of income transfers: Social Security (old age and survivor's benefits), veteran's payments, worker's compensation, unemployment compensation, cash assistance to poor families, disability insurance, and Supplemental Security Income. To receive income from the government, you or your family must meet some eligibility requirements, such as age, veteran status, employment status, disability, or income level. Nationwide, 41 percent of all families received some type of government transfer income in 1993. Of those receiving government cash transfers, the average payment was $8,633. (Appendix A includes a more detailed look at the type of government income families received.)

Contrary to public myth, single mothers are not receiving disproportionately large public "handouts." Though almost half of single mothers obtained government aid of some type, the average amount of such aid was $2,525. That only slightly exceeded the average of $1,970 received by nonelder two-adult families with children, and fell below the average of $2,546 received by families with two adults under the age of sixty-five with no children.

Other research confirms that government transfers—even need-based entitlement programs such as welfare—are spread widely through the population. Between 1976 and 1988, 24 percent of the population received cash entitlements (AFDC, General Assistance, or SSI), Food Stamps, or both. Not surprisingly, benefits most commonly went to the poorest—59 percent of the poorest tenth of the population got some cash entitlements. But more surprisingly, the programs reached well into the middle class: 23 percent of people in the middle tenth received need-based cash aid at some point during the twelve-year period.[1]

Interfamily transfers. The fourth way people get income is as a transfer from someone—usually a family member—not residing in the same household. When this transfer takes place among family members that live together, it is not recorded in annual income surveys. However, when parents no longer reside with their children and transfer income, for example, the government records this transaction as income for the receiving family. This type of transfer can take the form of child support, alimony, or gifts. Overall, a minuscule 6 percent of all families received interfamily transfers, with child support forming the largest component. Only 35 percent of all single-mother families received any child support. Among those who did, the average amount was $3,763. Comparatively, while just 8 percent of two-adult families with kids received this type of income, the average payments were about the same at $3,658.

On the average, child support and alimony represent a tiny fraction of family income. Even for single-mother families—the families to whom this support matters most—it amounts to only 8 percent of their income, an average of $1,308 per family in 1993. (This average is for all single-mother families, including those who received no child support.) Though the 1988 Family Support Act empowered states to pursue "deadbeat dads" more vigorously to extract child support, and while many states have adopted tough measures, the prospect of a child support bonanza for single mothers remains illusory. In many cases, the fathers themselves are poor and have little support to offer. Child support is simply too limited to serve as a primary source, or even much of a supplementary source, of income for poor single-mother families.

The family connection

Let's take a step back and summarize how family structure shapes family income. Several strong patterns emerge from Tables 3.2 and 3.3 as well as from Figure 3.3, which graphically restates the income sources obtained by each family type. The more adults in a family, the more income from wages and salaries. As adults pass retirement age, the family becomes less likely to earn wages and salaries, but much more likely to receive property and pension income along with government aid. Interestingly, the amount of government transfers does not vary much by family type. All the family types receive on average between $1,000 and $3,000 in government aid, with one exception: families with an adult aged sixty-five or older receive over $10,000 (largely in the form of Social Security). This is more than four times as much as single mothers and two-adult families without children, who tie for second place as recipients of government assistance.

Total income also follows a clear gender hierarchy. Lone women and single mothers make do with the least cash—by a wide margin. Lone women trail lone men by $4,000, and single mothers lag $9,000 behind single dads.

Figure 3.3 Income Sources for U.S. Families, 1993

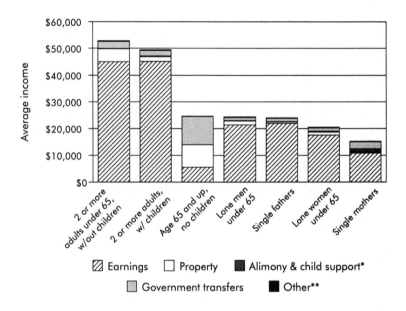

*Alimony and child support includes alimony, child support, and financial assistance not otherwise classified.

**Other income includes education aid and one-time income.

Source: Calculated by authors from U.S. Bureau of the Census, Current Population Survey, March1994.

Simply comparing dollar incomes does not, of course, take into account differences in families' needs. So when we compare a single older person's dollar income to that of a young family of eight, we overlook something important. A $25,000 salary may be adequate for a frugal person living alone, but supporting a large family on $25,000 would be quite a strain!

Adjusting income by the poverty line is a way to take these differing needs into account. The poverty line sets a minimum income threshold to meet basic needs for each family size and composition (the mix of children, persons over sixty-five, and younger adults in the family). In 1993, the poverty line for an

Figure 3.4   Income Sources for U.S. Families, Adjusted by the Poverty Line, 1993

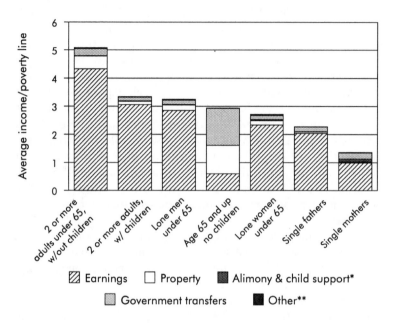

*Alimony and child support includes alimony, child support, and financial assistance not otherwise classified.

**Other income includes education aid and one-time income.

Source: Calculated by authors from U.S. Bureau of the Census, Current Population Survey, March1994.

elderly person living alone was $6,930, whereas the average poverty line for a family of eight was $24,838. While not a perfect measurement, the poverty line offers a well-known, consistent yardstick pegged to a family's basic needs.

Figure 3.4 puts the yardstick to work, depicting the amount each income source contributes to each family type—but this time, each family's income is divided by that family's poverty line income. For example, an income of "two" would mean the group of families has incomes that, on average, equal twice their poverty line incomes. We call this *need-adjusted income.*

When we apply this poverty-line yardstick to family incomes, we find that the average family of two or more adults with no kids had a family income over five times the poverty line, the average lone male had an income more than three times the poverty line, and the average single mother had income that stood just above the poverty line. We should note, however, that the adjustment just takes family size into account. It does not adjust for other special needs a family may have, such as those of a severely disabled family member or the high expenses of college tuition or childcare. Still, taking need into account in this limited way does alter the picture that emerges from family types' dollar incomes alone. Families of two adults with children, whose dollar incomes are much higher than those of lone men or elder families, fall to about the same level after adjusting for need. Lone males pull barely ahead of elders. But whether we look at dollar incomes or need-adjusted incomes, single mothers place dead last.

Single-mother families are much poorer than other families because all their potential sources of income are remarkably low. In terms of access to income, single mothers are female wage earners who must support nonwage (or very low-wage) earners —children—with only one adult to both work for pay and do the unpaid labor in the home. *All* single mothers face 1) family-sized income needs, 2) less time to work, and 3) a wage that is typically less than 70 percent of what men earn. Three strikes and you're not out, but you sure are likely to be down—on income! Unfortunately, government transfers, child support, and alimony fail to offset these disadvantages.

While only single mothers face this particular combination of obstacles to income, *all* women share similar problems. Perhaps most important, all women still face a labor market that on average rewards men more. Additionally, all women with young children, married or not, must often balance jobs and the time it takes to care for their kids—which affects their ability to get jobs and earn wages. These similarities make it useful to examine *all* women's wage-earning potential—a subject to which we now turn.

Notes

1. Howard Chernick, *Wide Cast for the Safety Net* (Washington, D.C.: Economic Policy Institute, 1995).

4

The Glass Ceiling
and the Sticky Floor:
Obstacles to Women
in the Workforce

Even the most highly educated, privileged women run into the "glass ceiling," the set of invisible barriers to advancement up the corporate ladder. For much larger numbers of working women—those laboring in "pink collar" jobs, such as secretary, waitress, or nursing aide—even the glass ceiling is out of sight. Instead, they experience the "sticky floor"—discriminatory hiring patterns that keep them concentrated at the bottom of the job scale. But despite differences, the glass ceiling and sticky floor share striking similarities. What plagues working mothers with a high school diploma also dogs highly qualified career women—a world that expects them to perform paid work without much regard to the time it takes to care for families, a world that expects them to put out equal, if not extra, effort without equal opportunity or compensation.

Who's making it in the labor market

To make it in the labor market, it helps to be male. Certainly, education helps improve earnings as well, but it helps women less. A glance at Table 4.1 confirms that when it comes to the dollar payoff for education, life most definitely is not fair.

Table 4.1   Unequal Payoffs
Hourly wage by education and gender, March 1994

	Men	Women	Female/male ratio
Less than 1st grade	$ 5.32	$ 4.47	.84
1st–8th grade	9.06	7.33	.81
High school dropout	8.28	6.31	.76
High school graduate	11.35	8.48	.75
College, less than Bachelor's	12.76	9.99	.78
Bachelor's degree	18.15	14.25	.79
Master's degree	20.35	17.80	.87
Professional degree	23.09	21.23	.92
All levels of education	13.32	10.46	.79

Source: Calculated by authors from U.S. Bureau of the Census, Current Population Survey, March 1994.

Overall, women average $10.46 per hour to men's $13.32 (the average includes part-time and part-year workers). Breaking wage levels down by education highlights the persistence of the pay gap. Women who dropped out of high school earn only one dollar an hour more than men who lack even a first grade education. A female high school graduate earns less than a male high school dropout. A bachelor's degree leaves women with wages closer to those of a man with an associate's degree than those of a man with a bachelor's. Women with a master's degree still don't catch up to males with only a bachelor's degree. On average, women in the workforce are actually slightly more educated than men—but no matter how far they scale the educational ladder, their pay lags behind.

The most important reason for these wage disparities is that men and women hold different kinds of jobs. As Table 4.2 shows, despite occupational shifts over the past twenty years, close to half of all employed women work in clerical and service jobs, compared to one-sixth of men. Thanks to affirmative action, women *have* entered managerial and professional ranks, and this helps account for the reduction of the gender gap from the mid-1970s onward. But within these upper-echelon jobs, women remain disproportionately concentrated among lower-

Table 4.2   Occupational Segregation Continues

Employed men and women by occupation, 1974 and 1994

Occupations as a percent of employed persons	Women		Men	
	1974	1994	1974	1994
Managerial	5.0%	12.4%	12.1%	14.0%
Professional	12.6%	16.3%	9.9%	12.5%
Technical	2.5%	3.6%	2.4%	2.8%
Sales	11.0%	12.8%	10.1%	11.4%
Administrative support	31.6%	26.0%	6.0%	5.9%
Service	20.6%	17.8%	8.1%	10.3%
Precision production, craft, and repair*	1.8%	2.2%	19.7%	18.4%
Operators, fabricators, and laborers**	13.3%	7.7%	24.4%	20.4%
Farming, forestry, and fishing	1.6%	1.2%	6.2%	4.4%
Total	100.0%	100.0%	100.0%	100.0%
Total employed (in thousands)	33,769	56,610	53,024	66,450

*Skilled workers in manufacturing and construction.

**Includes unskilled workers in manufacturing and construction.

Source: Diane E. Herz and Barbara H. Wootton, "Women in the Workforce: An Overview," in *The American Woman, 1996-97*, ed. Cynthia Costello and Barbara Kivimae Krimgold (New York: W.W. Norton and Company, 1996), table I-3.

level managers and lower-paid professionals (such as nurses and teachers, rather than doctors and lawyers). Women in the labor market continue to encounter both "glass ceilings" that block upward mobility and "sticky floors" that crowd them into low-paid jobs.[1]

Jobs with a future?

Occupational segregation will continue to dog women's job prospects into the future. According to projections by the U.S. Bureau of Labor Statistics, there will be growth in women's job opportunities—but low-paid jobs will provide the bulk of that growth.

Table 4.3   Fast Growing, Low Paying, Part 1

Projected 1992–2005 growth rate and current women's earnings for all industries and for industries that disproportionately hire women

Industry	Women as % of work-force, 1994	Projected employment growth, 1992–2005	Women's average annual earnings, 1993
All industries	46%	22%	$17,223
Retail trade	51	23	10,152
Finance, insurance, real estate	59	21	22,221
Services	62	47	17,582
Personal services	69	24	9,312
Personnel supply services	61	57	10,219
Health services	78	47	21,310
Educational services	68	27	17,982
Social services	81	89	16,797
Government	43	18	24,222

Source: *Statistical Abstract*, 1995, tables 653–54; calculated by authors from U.S. Bureau of the Census, Current Population Survey, March 1994.

Breaking job growth down by industry (see Table 4.3), we consider the four broad industry groups that employ the highest percentages of women: retail trade, finance/insurance/real estate, services, and government. The two industries where women earn better wages—government and finance—will grow more slowly than overall employment, shrinking as a percentage of the workforce. Service jobs, which offer lower earnings (just barely above women's average of $17,200), will grow rapidly, and trade jobs—the lowest paid of all—will slightly exceed overall job growth. Services, of course, are a mixed bag: the health and education industries provide relatively decent jobs for women, but their predicted growth rates do not match the spurts projected for lower-paying social services and personnel supply (the industry that includes temporary help agencies).

Occupational growth projections tell much the same story (Table 4.4). Certain "women's" jobs are growing rapidly. But

Table 4.4   Fast Growing, Low Paying, Part 2

Selected fast-growing occupations with projected 1992–2005 growth rate and current median weekly earnings of full-time workers

Occupation	Projected employment growth, 1991–2005	Women's median weekly earnings (full-time workers), 1995
All occupations	22%	$406
Home health aides*	138	285
Personal and home care aides*	130	193
Childcare workers	66	182
Legal secretaries	57	395
Nursing aides, orderlies, attendants	45	275
Food preparation workers	43	263
Registered nurses	42	693
Waiters and waitresses	36	258
Receptionists and information clerks	34	336

*These are two of the three occupations projected by the Bureau of Labor Statistics to be the fastest-growing in the country. The third is "human services workers"; our source does not give earnings for this occupation.

Sources: *Statistical Abstract*, 1995, tables 650–51; Bureau of Labor Statistics, *Employment and Earnings*, January 1996, table 39. In cases where earnings for a specific occupation are not reported, earnings for a closely related occupation are substituted.

many are pink-collar jobs that pay low wages and generally offer only part-time hours or part-year employment. The 800,000 nurses projected to join the workforce between 1992 and 2005 will be more than offset by the 600,000 waiters and waitresses and 600,000 nursing aides. Many, though not all, of the fastest-growing occupations that are most accessible to women offer earnings that simply fall below the survival level—even for full-time workers.

Silent depression

Compounding the effects of the glass ceiling and sticky floor on women's wages is the ongoing economic stagnation—the "silent depression" stalking the United States, as economist Wallace Peterson calls it. While unemployment has dropped from the highs of the 1980s, wage growth has continued to lag behind inflation, and jobs have become less secure.

Consider the unemployment problem. As of 1996, the U.S. unemployment rate stood at 5.4 percent—7.2 million people. Some economists seek to characterize this level as "full employment"—and it certainly comes as a relief after recessions that drove unemployment up to 10 percent in 1982 and 7 percent in 1992. Still, today's joblessness stands well above the unemployment rates for much of the 1960s, which fell as low as 3.5 percent in 1969. Furthermore, the unemployment rate hides the true level of labor market distress. The official rate does not count as unemployed:

1. "discouraged workers" who still want a job, but have recently given up looking due to a poor job market;
2. involuntary part-time workers, who would prefer full-time hours (a total of 4.5 million workers in 1995!);
3. people available for work, but not looking due to family, school, or health issues;
4. people who want a job, but have not looked in the last year; and
5. the enormous U.S. prison population—we incarcerate people at ten times the rate of European countries, keeping them off the streets and out of unemployment lines.

In 1994, for example, the official unemployment rate was 6 percent. By simply adding in the first two categories and counting each involuntary part-time worker as "half" of an unemployed person, unemployment would have jumped to 8 percent. If we incorporate all five groups in an "*under*employment rate," this time counting each involuntary part-timer as one underemployed person, we find that 15 percent of the workforce is underemployed.[2] Furthermore, some groups of the underemployed—particularly involuntary part-time workers—are growing faster than the workforce as a whole, causing the official unemployment rate to fall farther and farther behind the *under*employment rate over time.

Of course, even the official unemployment rate is much higher for some than for others. In 1996, blacks and Latinos were almost twice as likely to be unemployed as the average worker; teens were almost three times as likely to be jobless. (Women's unemployment rate was exactly equal to the national average.) And joblessness followed a patchwork pattern across the country. In a March 1997 snapshot, unemployment rates ranged from a low of 2.1 percent in booming New Hampshire to a high of 7.8 percent in struggling Alaska and Washington, D.C., with depression levels of 13 percent and higher in the California communities of Bakersfield, Fresno, Salinas, and Modesto, as well as some parts of Texas.[3]

Unemployment only tells part of the grim economic story. In addition, wages have grown too slowly to keep up with rising prices: real hourly wages for nonsupervisory workers in the private sector, after adjusting for inflation, dropped 13 percent between 1973 and 1996.[4] Since earnings inequality has widened, those at the bottom—especially the less educated—have done much worse than the average. And as the headlines about corporate downsizing telegraph, all jobs are becoming more temporary or "contingent." Shortly after announcing layoffs of 40,000 employees in early 1996, AT&T Vice President for Human Resources James Meadows explained that "People need to look at themselves as self-employed, as vendors who come to this company to sell their skills. In AT&T, we have to promote the whole concept of the workforce being contingent, though most of the contingent workers are inside our walls." "Jobs," Meadows added, are being replaced by "projects" or "fields of work."[5] Between unemployment, slipping wage levels, and disappearing job security, the overall economic landscape remains discouraging.

Families on the uneven playing field

To understand the implications of gender inequality in the labor market for *families*, it is necessary to focus on the primary adults (family heads and their spouses) whose paychecks sustain them. Looking at these breadwinners, we can explore how having children and being married alter workforce outcomes for men and women.

Tables 4.5 and 4.6 illustrate the uneven economic playing field from a family perspective. Table 4.5 looks at the hourly wages and the average number of hours worked per year by pri-

Table 4.5   Who Gets the Wages, Who Works the Hours

Men's and women's average hourly wages and hours worked per year, by presence of children and number of adults (and adjusted for age differences), 1993–1994*

Family type	Average hourly wages	Average hours worked/year**
Women with children:		
Two-adult families	$10.91	851
One-adult families	9.77	810
Women without children:		
Two-adult families	11.28	1,128
One-adult families	11.67	1,281
Men with children		
Two-adult families	14.71	1,776
One-adult families	13.12	1,457
Men without children		
Two-adult families	14.96	1,642
One-adult families	13.21	1,452

*Data are for men and women who are the head or the spouse of the head of a household only. Wage and hours figures are computed holding constant any effects of age differences among the various groups. Wage figures are for March 1994; hours figures are 1993 annual hours.

**Includes all those who have worked any hours. For reference, a year-round, full-time job typically is 2,000 hours per year.

Source: Calculated by authors from U.S. Bureau of the Census, Current Population Survey, March 1994.

mary adults. We have controlled for age differences in order to directly examine the effects of having children under age eighteen in the household.

Women with children earn somewhat less per hour than those without children and a lot less than men; they also work many fewer hours than women without children. Men, meanwhile, earn several dollars per hour more than women in every category, and work many more hours. For men, having children has little effect on wages earned—presumably because men are far

Table 4.6 Unequal Opportunities

Men's and women's average hourly wages, by presence of children, number of adults, and race (and adjusted for age differences), March 1994*

Family type	Non-Latino white	Black	Latino
Women with children:			
Two-adult families	$11.03	$10.28	$ 9.95
One-adult families	10.07	9.55	9.13
Women without children:			
Two-adult families	11.34	10.21	10.78
One-adult families	12.17	10.22	7.61
Men with children			
Two-adult families	15.36	13.02	10.03
One-adult families	13.34	**	**
Men without children			
Two-adult families	15.26	13.54	10.80
One-adult families	13.73	12.16	8.82

*Data are for men and women who are the head or the spouse of the head of a household only. Wage figures are computed holding constant any effects of age differences among the various groups.

**Numbers are so small as to be statistically unreliable in this sample.

Source: Calculated by authors from U.S. Bureau of the Census, Current Population Survey, March 1994.

less involved in caring for children—but it does seem to affect hours worked—presumably because men with children are more involved in earning income.

Marriage, on the other hand, has a large impact on men's work patterns, but not on women's. Married men (or, more accurately, men with another adult in the family) work more hours and earn higher wages. But on average, women with children under eighteen work very similar hours regardless of whether or not they are married—though single mothers reap lower wages. Married mothers do spend forty-one more hours per year working for pay than single mothers. This difference, however, is reversed if we consider only mothers with children aged six and up: single mothers log 1,336 annual hours to married mothers' 1,266 hours.

All of these differences add up. Looking at the two wage extremes, married men with children receive 50 percent more for every hour they work than single mothers.

Race matters as well (Table 4.6). Black and Latina women earn less than white women, regardless of marital status or the presence of children. Black and Latino men also suffer a wage penalty. Within *every* racial and ethnic group, women earn lower wages than men, and in most cases, women with children earn less than other women, with single mothers usually earning the least of all.

A poverty of time

The fewer hours and lower earnings of women with children are one reflection of the growing tug-of-war between work and family. As more and more women work outside the home, families face escalating burn out. Especially for families with children, important and unavoidable duties must be performed for households to function. Children of all ages need care, food must be bought and prepared, houses cleaned and maintained, bills paid, and family members clothed. This all takes time—and money. And despite the fact that work done in the home has no *market* value when family members do it, it is extremely valuable work. If the work is not done adequately, neglected family members pay the price first, and often society ends up paying as well.

How much time is involved in taking care of families? One recent estimate puts the average time women spend in household work at fifty hours a week.[6] In a recent survey of working men and women who have spouses (or partners), working women with children reported spending an average of sixty-one hours a week on household duties that included childcare and chores, while working men reported putting in forty-six hours a week on the same set of tasks.[7] For poor families, routine household tasks claim even more time (see "Time vs. Money," page 55).

TIME VS. MONEY

Remember the old adage "time equals money"? It refers to the cost of wasting time. But the equation also runs the other way: if you have more money, you can save yourself some time by paying for services you don't have to do yourself. For example, at the end of a busy day, many of us would rather buy a take-out dinner than take the time to cook it ourselves.

People with high-paying jobs and long hours tend to buy many of the services a "wife" used to do at home. But for poor families, the time vs. money tradeoff is much more difficult. Without enough money—even when doing paid work—some relatively simple and necessary chores take more time. The list below highlights some of the differences in how a well-off vs. financially pinched family might meet some common household needs.

Need	Well-off family	Financially pinched family
Clothing	Buying new clothes, some from pricey catalogs	Combing through second-hand clothes and mending clothes
Meals	Buying food at the most convenient market or eating out	Searching for bargains or standing in line at the food pantry
Laundry	Doing at home with own washer and dryer, or taking to dry cleaner	Taking clothes to the laundromat
Transportation	Driving one of the family's new, well-maintained cars	Relying on public transport, nursing a clunker car, or arranging a ride
Budgeting	Having enough savings to splurge with the urge; using a checking account, credit card, or ATM to pay bills conveniently	Struggling to figure out how to make the money last through the week (or month); robbing Peter to pay Paul; paying bills in person, purchasing money orders

It is easy to see how much longer the financially strapped family spends on meeting their needs than the well-off family. Money equals time.

Childcare responsibilities claim most of women's home work time. Even women who work outside the home and presumably find childcare arrangements reported spending an average of thirty-seven hours a week taking care of children—the equivalent of another full-time job. For working couples without children, the professed work time at home falls by thirty to forty hours, to an average of twenty-three hours for women and seventeen hours for men.[8]

The cost of children

The costs of having and raising children are high. First, there are the direct costs—housing, clothing, medical care, and childcare. Based on a recent survey of childcare centers, full-time care for a preschool child ranges from $217 a month (or $2,604 annually) in Mobile, Alabama, to $589 monthly (or $7,068 per year) in New York City (Table 4.7). By way of comparison, the 1996 poverty line for a single individual was $7,740! A different survey of parents yielded a national average of $300 per month (or $3,600 per year) for full-time preschool care.[9] After-school care for a school-age child costs one-third to one-half as much, averaging $115 per month in a 1988 survey, and $185 per month in a 1990 survey—still a big chunk out of most family budgets.[10] For many families, childcare is as expensive—and as necessary, if adult members have jobs—as rent. For poor families, the burden is a heavy one: poor families with a preschool child and an employed mother who pays for child care spend almost one-quarter of their income on childcare.[11]

Health care is another substantial cost for working parents. Those fortunate enough to have employer-sponsored health insurance typically pay some portion of that expense, which is much higher for family coverage. The average family health plan required $118 per month in employee contributions in 1994.[12] On top of this, the National Health Care Expenditure Survey estimated that children under six add an average of about $200 per year in out-of-pocket health care costs, while children aged six to eighteen average almost $300.[13]

The data in Table 4.8 illustrate how expensive it is to maintain a single-mother household with children. The table summarizes three recent estimates of basic, no-frills minimum budgets for a

Table 4.7   Childcare Costs Coast to Coast
Monthly daycare costs for a preschool child, 1995

Location	Monthly daycare cost
Most expensive	
New York, NY	$589
Boston, MA	579
Minneapolis, MN	537
Philadelphia, PA	506
Washington, DC	486
Manchester, NC	469
Wilmington, DE	460
Chicago, IL	455
Anchorage, AK	454
Hartford, CT	445
Least expensive	
Mobile, AL	$217
Casper, WY	217
Jackson, MS	231
Tampa, FL	246
New Orleans, LA	256
Columbia, SC	263
Little Rock, AR	266
Billings, MT	280
Boise, ID	285
Springfield, IL	285

Note: Daycare costs are based on monthly fees for a three-year-old child in a for-profit daycare center, five days a week, eight hours a day. The locations are in representative suburban locations within these metropolitan areas.

Source: "Consumerscope," *Consumer's Digest* (January/February 1996): 6. From Runzheimer International, Runzheimer Park, Rochester, WI 53167-0009.

woman with two children—one for a large eastern city, one for a midwestern farm state, and one for a rural New England state.

To make the minimum monthly payments, a family must earn $13,900 in Boston, $10,600 in Nebraska, and $11,724 in Maine *before one penny goes to payroll taxes or other costs of going to work* (childcare, transportation, or health care costs). Adding in the costs of working nearly doubles the amount required: a Boston family now needs $25,500, a Nebraska family $18,400, and

Table 4.8   Basic Costs of Maintaining a Family

Monthly costs for a woman with two children in Boston, Massachusetts, the state of Nebraska, and the state of Maine

Basic costs	Boston	Nebraska	Maine
Unavoidable minimum costs			
Housing and utilities*	$713	$466	$508
Food	382	240	310
Clothing and miscellaneous**	—	122	81
Transportation (other than work)***	64	53	79
Subtotal	1,159	881	977
Added costs of going to work			
Childcare****	646	360	359
Health care*****	214	201	166
Transportation to work	106	88	49
Subtotal	966	649	574
Total	$2,125	$1,530	$1,551

*Includes housing, heat, phone, and electricity.

**Information not available for Boston.

***Transportation costs in Boston are assumed to be at the national average. In all locations, nonwork transportation is assumed to be 60 percent of the distance traveled to work. For Maine, estimates are based on owning a used car (commuting to work on public transportation is not an option for most Maine workers) and do not include savings to purchase another used car.

****Childcare costs in Boston are based on one four-year-old and one school-age child requiring after-school care. Costs in Nebraska are based on a weighted average of children's ages. Costs in Maine are based on one child under six and one school-age child requiring after-school care.

*****Health care costs are assumed to be completely covered by Medicaid for non-working mothers (a rather generous assumption). Health care costs in Massachusetts are set at the national average. Costs in all locations assume that the employee pays 30 percent of the insurance premium.

Sources: Massachusetts Human Service Coalition, *Up the Down Staircase* (Boston: 1993), Boston figures for 1992; Patricia Funk, *Economic Self-Sufficiency: The Minimum Cost of Family Support in Nebraska, 1994* (Lincoln: Nebraska Center for Legal Services, 1994); Stephanie Seguino, *Living on the Edge: Women Working and Providing for Families in the Maine Economy, 1993* (Orono, ME: Margaret Chase Smith Center for Public Policy, 1995); additional calculations by authors.

a Maine family $18,612 to scrape by once the mother goes to work. Yet a worker earning the 1997 minimum wage of $5.15 an hour working year-round, full-time only makes $10,300 per year before taxes. Even a woman whose wage equals the nationwide single mother average of $9.71 an hour only earns $20,200 a year—enough to survive in Nebraska or Maine, but not in Boston. (Nebraska and Maine *wages*, as well as costs, fall below the national average, so single mothers in these states are less likely to earn this much.)

In addition to the direct costs of raising a family, children impose indirect costs. Raising young children used to be widely considered a full-time job. With women's desire and need to enter the labor force, raising small children is now part of the "double day" for many women and, increasingly, men. That is, women work outside the home for pay and then do a considerable amount of unpaid work. To accomplish this, women (and more and more men) need jobs with a great deal of flexibility. Women with young children typically work part-time and try to find jobs located close to their childcare provider. But flexibility usually comes at a cost—lower wages and fewer benefits.

The most obvious indirect cost of a part-time job is the lost income resulting from the shorter work week. But part-time work also pays about 40 percent less per hour than a full-time job, and about half of that wage gap persists even for similar workers in similar jobs.[14] So a twenty-hour-a-week job does not usually pay half as much as a comparable forty-hour-a-week job —instead, the average part-time job offers less than one-third the weekly wage of a full-time job. Further, part-time jobs almost never come with fringe benefits. About 22 percent of part-timers receive health insurance as a benefit, compared to 78 percent of full-time workers. Only 26 percent of part-time workers get pension coverage, whereas 60 percent of their full-time counterparts enjoy such coverage.[15]

Shorter hours are not the only flexibility parents need in jobs. Typically, they need to find work and childcare in locations that are close to each other. In a day filled with paid and unpaid work, there is little time for traveling to and from work—especially when emergencies come up involving children. This limits the pool of available jobs. In a recent Los Angeles area survey, 30

percent of women reported that in the last year, childcare constraints had caused them not to look for or apply for a job; another 10 percent turned down a job they had been offered, and
6 percent quit or were fired from a job due to childcare issues.[16]
Even those mothers who have successfully made their way
into full-time, high-status jobs still face significant barriers. Full-
time jobs—at least those that pay well—often assume there is a
"wife" at home doing large amounts of unpaid work. When professional women who do not have "wives" find they cannot work
more than forty hours a week, they are often shunted aside to
the so-called "mommy track." Women's responsibilities at home,
in addition to gender discrimination at the workplace, limit their
ability to be promoted to the highest echelons of their workplaces. They hit the glass ceiling. Although women make up 46
percent of the workforce, only 5 percent of senior managers in
Fortune 2,000 industrial and service companies are women![17]
In the United States, individual families—in particular, mothers—bear the costs of having and raising children. Until 1993,
the United States had no national parental leave policy. Even
now, the law only stipulates that employers with fifty or more
employees must allow parents to take up to twelve weeks of *unpaid* leave from their jobs. Many workplaces slip below this
law's threshold: nationwide, 43 percent of the workforce is in
establishments employing fewer than fifty people.
Few employers provide on-site childcare centers or directly
subsidize care. Further, there is *no* serious national policy re-
garding the provision of childcare or the cost of raising children.
Although the government provides a small childcare block grant
allotment and limited childcare subsidies to poor mothers receiving cash assistance who are in training or work programs,
the closest the United States comes to substantial child-income
policies are three provisions in the income tax code: the exemption for children, the deduction for childcare expenses (both of
which apply only to those who owe taxes), and the Earned Income Credit, a refundable credit for families. States provide daycare subsidies for some low-income mothers, but this assistance
remains skimpy. Consider Massachusetts, often viewed as a
leader in social services. In early 1996, the state provided only
4,000 daycare slots for children from low-income families, plus
18,000 for children of mothers in the jobs program for AFDC

recipients. But there were over 412,000 children aged five and under in the state—86,000 of them in poor families.

In addition to the burdens of being a parent, women face earnings problems precisely because they are women. The remainder of this chapter discusses how that gender gap combines with nationwide employment trends to narrow women's job options.

Cycle of dependency:
How business, government, and families
depend on women's paid and unpaid labor

On the whole, women's increased participation in the paid labor force has been a mixed blessing. On the one hand, in a culture that puts such a high premium on earning ability, consumerism, and economic independence, the ability to earn income affords U.S. working women more respect and choices than ever before. Women's wholesale entrance into the labor market has broken down many of the barriers between men and women: it is more common to see women and men as equals at work, and for both men and women to share the work of caring for children. On the other hand, the increase in women's labor participation raises expectations that all women can and should work and means that more women work the "double day." For the first time in U.S. history, most childless women can earn enough on their own to support themselves without the help of a father or a husband. Yet since women's wages are still lower than men's on average, they usually cannot support themselves *and* others without another adult's income. It now typically takes *two* adult workers to support children.

In short, women's increased labor force participation has brought some personal liberation, but has also significantly changed the economic turf. In just a few decades, we have gone from a society in which married women were not expected to work to one in which women—regardless of their marital status —anticipate almost a lifetime of paid work, both because they want it and, increasingly, because they need it.

But with everybody working, who's supposed to care for children? Neither business nor government has accommodated the social revolution in women's economic roles by reducing the

work week, providing daycare for workers, or giving child subsidies to all families, regardless of their structure. Instead, families, businesses, and government are trapped in a cycle of dependency on women's unpaid labor.

That cycle now includes dependency on women's *paid* work
as well. In fact, both business and government have used the
expectation that women will work outside the home to squeeze
more work for less pay out of families by keeping both men's
and women's wages down. Men's falling wages (after adjusting
for inflation) have been made up by family members—typically
women—working more hours. But when women enter the labor
force to offset men's lost wages, this action accommodates the
lower wages. Ironically, the corporate structure has absorbed
many of women's new-found gains, resulting in a family wage
system in which two adult earners are the standard. This, in
turn, causes an acute family speed-up: like Alice in Wonderland,
families must work harder to stay in the same place. To be sure,
the old system geared toward the single male breadwinner had
its problems, but it at least afforded certain numbers of men and
women the time to take care of their families.

Meanwhile, politicians have exploited the expectation that
women will work for pay to justify slashing government aid to
single mothers. Since there already are not enough jobs for everyone who wants one, the idea that all single mothers should
and can find jobs is hardly realistic. Nonetheless, the new rules
of the game either reduce single mothers' government-provided
compensation for the work of caring for their children or require
them to perform additional work—or both.

For working women (and, increasingly, men) with children,
neither the job structure nor the government provides much
support for the time-consuming and important work of caring
for families. The bottom line is that women are expected to
work, but their labor market opportunities remain severely limited. Caring for children and other family members imposes a
steep cost in time and money. The gender gap in wages continues to yawn. And even in what is touted as a robust U.S. economy, unemployment and a shortage of good jobs still stymie
many job seekers —and will do so for the foreseeable future.
These labor market hurdles loom large for all women, but they

loom largest of all for single mothers. In the next chapter, we shed light on the "bottomless pit" to examine the problems and survival strategies of single mothers.

Notes

1. These issues are documented and discussed in the reports and recommendations issued by the Glass Ceiling Commission created as part of the Civil Rights Act of 1991 and housed at the U.S. Department of Labor. See in particular Lois Shaw, Dell Champlin, Heidi Hartmann, and Roberta Spalter-Roth, *The Impact of the Glass Ceiling and Structural Change on Minorities and Women,* 1993. Retrieved electronically from ftp.ilr.cornell.edu.
2. See Marc Breslow and Matthew Howard, "The Real Un(der)employment Rate," *Dollars and Sense* (May/June 1995). The estimates reported here include additional calculations by the authors.
3. U.S. Bureau of Labor Statistics, "Unemployment Rates by State and Selected Metropolitan Areas," from web site stats.bls.gov/news.release/laus.nws.htm (1997).
4. U.S. Council of Economic Advisors, *Economic Report of the President* (1997), table B-45.
5. Edmund L. Andrews, "Don't Go Away Mad, Just Go Away: Can AT&T Be the Nice Guy as It Cuts 40,000 Jobs?" *New York Times,* 13 February 1996, pp. D1-10.
6. Juliet Schor, *The Overworked American* (New York: Basic Books, 1992).
7. Ellen Galinsky, James T. Bond, and Dana Friedman, *The National Study of the Changing Workforce* (New York: Families and Work Institute, 1993).
8. Ibid.
9. Unpublished tabulation from the Survey of Income and Program Participation, 1993, provided by Lynne Casper, U.S. Bureau of the Census, Population Division.
10. Dale Borman Fink, "School-Age Child Care in America: Findings of a 1988 Study," Action Research Paper #3 (Wellesley, MA: Center for Research on Women, 1990); Sandra L. Hofferth, April Brayfield, Sharon Deich, and Pamela Holcomb, *The National Child Care Survey, 1990,* Report 91-5 (Washington, D.C.: Urban Institute Press, 1991). Estimate of $185 monthly comes from Table 3.2 average cost figure of $2.65 per hour for mothers working full-time, multiplied by average hours figure of 16.1 hours per week, multiplied by 4.33 weeks per month.
11. Sandra L. Hofferth, April Brayfield, Sharon Deich, and Pamela Holcomb, *The National Child Care Survey, 1990,* Report 91-5 (Washington, D.C.: Urban Institute Press, 1991).
12. Based on 1988 estimate by the Congressional Research Service, as reported in National Health Care Campaign, *The Affordability of Health*

Care for Nebraska's Working Families (Washington, D.C.: December 1989). This estimate is extended to 1994 by applying the Consumer Price Index for medical care costs.

13. See Trudi J. Renwick and Barbara R. Bergmann, "A Budget-Based Definition of Poverty with an Application to Single-Parent Families," *Journal of Human Resources*, vol. 28, no. 1 (1993).

14. Chris Tilly, *Half a Job: Bad and Good Part-Time Jobs in a Changing Labor Market* (Philadelphia: Temple University Press, 1996), pp. 53-59.

15. James Rebitzer, *The Demand for Part-Time Workers: Theory, Evidence, and Policy Implications* (Washington, D.C.: Economic Policy Institute, 1987).

16. Julie E. Press, "A Matrix of Constraints: Urban Labor Markets at the Intersection of Gender, Race and Class Inequality" (Ph.D. diss., University of California, Los Angeles, forthcoming 1997).

17. Liz Hren, "Policy Perspective: The 11/95 Report of the Federal Glass Ceiling Commission," *Policy Perspectives* (Cambridge, MA: Radcliffe Public Policy Institute), Spring 1996: 4.

5

Bottomless Pits:
Why Single Mothers
Fare Worst

Single mothers have always been poor. Four decades ago, in 1959, 60 percent of single-mother families were poor, compared to 16 percent of other families with children. As of 1993, 52 percent of single-mother families lived in poverty, as opposed to 11 percent of other families with children. Having examined the impact of family structure and gender on incomes and expenses, it is easy to see the three basic reasons why single-mother families are so poor. Together, they act as a "triple whammy."

Triple whammy

Part 1: The gender wage gap The first strike against single mothers is that the one working-age adult in the family is a woman. While the vast majority of women who work can support themselves, only about half can support an entire family. The Institute for Women's Policy Research found that, nationwide, 45 percent of all women would earn too little to bring a family of three up to the poverty threshold (including daycare costs for one child), *even if they worked full-time, year-round.*[1]

Part 2: Cradles to rock Having children affects mothers' work—both paid and unpaid. To obtain the flexibility they need in paid work, mothers must sacrifice pay and job variety. While all mothers are disproportionately crowded into "women's jobs," single mothers face particularly powerful occupational segregation: of those in the paid workforce in 1993, 44 percent worked in clerical jobs and 27 percent in service occupations —a total of 71 percent. By comparison, 46 percent of mothers in two-adult families hold clerical jobs and 18 percent occupy service jobs, totaling 64 percent.[2] The big difference here is that single mothers are far more likely to end up in service occupations, the lowest-wage "women's" jobs, since childcare demands constrain their choices even more.

Part 3: Not enough hands The simple fact is that families with more adults can earn more. Single-mother families, by definition, have one adult to both earn income and take care of children. While this is true of single-father families as well, fathers' earning power as men offsets some of the difficulty.

New choices, old problems

A growing proportion of women are single mothers. This increase holds for black, white, and Latino women; for middle-class as well as poor women; and in all parts of the country. In fact, the trend is also growing in Europe—and the United States is far from the extreme case. In Denmark, for example, births out of wedlock increased from 8 percent of all births in 1960 to 45 percent in 1988. Out-of-wedlock birth rates in France, Britain, Norway, and Sweden all exceed U.S. rates.[3] Of course, having a child out of wedlock is only one source of single motherhood; separation, divorce, and the death of a spouse are others. Only one-quarter of U.S. single parents have never been married.

In the United States, among black women who completed eighth grade or less, the percentage of single mothers with children under eighteen nearly doubled between 1960 and 1987, from 29 to 56 percent. Among white women with sixteen or more years of education, the percentage *more than* doubled in the same time—from 5 to 11 percent.[4] Indeed, in relative terms, the chances of being a single mother grew considerably faster for white women. In 1970, 44 percent of out-of-wedlock births were to white women; by 1991, that figure had risen to 58 percent.[5] Nationwide, the growth in single motherhood continues, although the pace has slowed. Between 1970 and 1980, the proportion of children living with single mothers rose from 11 to 18 percent; between 1980 and 1990, that proportion climbed more slowly to 22 percent, creeping up to 23 percent as of 1993.[6]

Why are more women becoming single mothers? Certainly not because raising children as a single mother is easy—as we have seen, half of all single mothers and their children live in poverty even *after* taking government cash assistance into account. But women have more choices than they once did. Divorce has become easier, tolerance for domestic violence has decreased, and it is far more socially acceptable for a woman to raise a child alone.

Men have more choices, too, with fewer strictures against divorce or abandonment, and fewer pressures to marry the mothers of their children. And while on average a woman and her children experience a decrease in their standard of living upon divorce, the ex-husband sees an increase in his. In 1992, almost two out of every five divorced mothers and their children were poor.[7] In fact, divorce is the most common trigger for catastrophic income losses among women aged twenty-six to thirty-five, accounting for one-quarter of large-scale income drops—far outdistancing the layoff or death of a family member, or *any* other cause of economic disaster.[8]

The shifting patterns of labor force participation and wages have also influenced family structure. As more women become economically active in the paid labor force, their ability to be self-sufficient increases, making marriage less of an economic necessity. Men's falling wages have also contributed to diminishing marriage rates. Men are reluctant to get married when their incomes are low—although they do not seem to be hesitant to become fathers.[9]

Is a single mother a bad mother?

In the current political climate, many are prepared to brand single mothers as bad mothers. This is unfair. To be sure, single mothers face a formidable set of economic obstacles, as we have just outlined. And these economic disadvantages have costs for their children. But single mothers have their reasons for being single—reasons that include domestic violence; high rates of male unemployment, incarceration, and early death in the poor communities where single motherhood is most common; and the simple inability to find the right match. Denouncing single mothers as a group implies that if only they could find a man— any man—they and their children would be better off. This preposterous claim potentially leads to a distasteful set of policy proposals, including forced marriage or the forced removal of children from single mothers, regardless of their ability to parent. Instead, we should acknowledge that poverty, not single motherhood, is the problem.

One source of confusion is that discussions often tangle single motherhood with welfare recipiency, teen pregnancy, and bearing children out of wedlock. Although there are overlaps, these are *not* all the same thing, nor do they involve the same group of people. Prior to the elimination of the AFDC program in 1996, only one-third of single mothers received AFDC, only one AFDC household in twelve was headed by a teen mother, and only one-quarter of single mothers were never married. Outof-wedlock births have increased among all women, not just among those eligible for welfare, and women of all income groups are less likely to marry and stay married. While the childbearing rates of single women have changed very little, single women are now a larger percentage of all women, so births to single women are a larger percentage of all births.[10] Despite a large volume of research, the myths persist, holding that teen pregnancy is an epidemic (while in actuality, teen birth rates are declining) and that overly generous welfare benefits encourage unwed motherhood (in fact, research shows no connection). Table 5.1 takes on some of these myths (as does Appendix B).

These days, the attacks don't stop with unwed mothers—they extend to divorced mothers as well. But the claims that divorce is bad for children don't take into account the possibility that they might have fared worse if their parents remained together in a loveless, angry, or even violent marriage.[11]

Indeed, poverty and the public stigma that has always been attached to public assistance are far more harmful to children than their mother's marital status. The most important factor accounting for the difficulties experienced by children from single-mother families, divorced or otherwise, is low income.[12] Just

Table 5.1   Debunking the Myths

MYTH: *Births to teen mothers are the primary cause of poverty.*

FACT: Many teen mothers live in poor families in poor neighborhoods and have access only to poor schools. A study controlling for these factors by comparing girls from the same family found that those who postponed pregnancy were not significantly more likely to finish high school, get married, or escape poverty than their sisters who bore children during their teen years.[13] A large percentage (42 percent) of women who receive welfare had their first children when they were teens, but that percentage has not changed in twenty years.[14]

MYTH: *Teen motherhood is out of control.*

FACT: In 1993, about 7 percent of mothers were unwed teenagers, while their kids represented less than 1 percent of all children living in related families.[15] Only about 8 percent of all welfare households are headed by teen mothers.[16] Teen birth rates are declining. In 1970, there were about sixty-eight births per thousand teenage women; by 1990, there were about sixty. The percentage born out of wedlock has increased because marriage has become less common throughout society.[17] Between 1982 and 1992, birth rates for unmarried mothers increased faster among women ages twenty to thirty-nine than among teenagers.[18]

MYTH: *Welfare causes an increase in out-of-wedlock births.*

FACT: Research consistently shows that receiving welfare does not significantly increase out-of-wedlock births. In June 1994, seventy-six prominent researchers in the areas of poverty, the labor market, and family structure signed a statement refuting the notion that welfare is the main cause of rising out-of-wedlock births. The signers represented a variety of major institutions, disciplines, and political viewpoints, and included nearly all the major researchers in the fields.[19]

MYTH: *Lowering benefit levels will reduce out-of-wedlock births.*

FACT: New Jersey's benefit package is 58 percent higher than Mississippi's, yet the rates of single parenthood in these two states are the same. Mississippi and Alabama have the lowest welfare benefit levels in the nation, yet their teen birth rates are among the highest.[20] Further, the value of cash benefits plus Food Stamps has declined over the same period that out-of-wedlock births have increased. In the mid-1980s, Canada's public assistance programs for poor single mothers provided benefits almost twice as high as those in the United States, but out-of-wedlock birth rates there remained far lower.[21]

Source: Excerpted from Randy Albelda, Nancy Folbre, and the Center for Popular Economics, *The War on the Poor* (New York: The New Press, 1996), with permission of the authors.

as poverty and unemployment make it harder to provide for basic needs, they also put strains on marriages and family life. Poor two-parent families are almost twice as likely to break up as are two-parent families that aren't poor.[22]

Families cannot simply be defined in demographic terms—the quality of relationships is what matters most for children's well-being. Many "traditional" families experience domestic violence or child neglect. About two-thirds of women receiving public assistance have been sexually or physically abused as adults.[23] Indeed, being poor, more than living in any particular type of family, increases the incidence of child abuse.[24] Because it has been the only public safety net for women and children, welfare has served as a vital avenue for them to escape abusive relationships.

Beyond Murphy Brown: Differences among single mothers

While single mothers as a group face formidable economic disadvantages, single mothers are *not* all the same. Few indeed look like Murphy Brown—white, highly educated, and affluent. But neither are single mothers primarily black or primarily welfare recipients. Close to two-thirds of single mothers in 1993 were white, and over two-thirds did *not* receive AFDC during that year. Comparing AFDC recipients with nonrecipients provides some clues as to why those who opt for welfare have little alternative (see Table 5.2).

The single mothers who received AFDC in 1993 looked very different from those who didn't. They were less educated and younger—both factors leading to lower wage potential. Recipient mothers were more likely to be Latina or black and subject to racial discrimination or job segregation that further depresses earnings. They more commonly lived in a large city or rural area—again, locations associated with reduced earning opportunities.

Furthermore, AFDC recipients faced more constraints on their working time than did single mothers not receiving aid. As Table 5.2 shows, recipient mothers were much more likely to have young children—a factor that makes it difficult to do large

Table 5.2 Differences That Make a Difference

Profile of single mothers who received AFDC, single mothers who didn't, and married mothers, 1993

Characteristic	Single mothers receiving AFDC	Single mothers not receiving AFDC	Married mothers
Education			
High school dropouts	39.8%	22.2%	13.5%
High school grads	37.5%	36.0%	35.1%
With post-HS education	22.9%	41.9%	51.3%
Average age (years)	30.6	37.1	36.6
Black	44.3%	30.3%	7.9%
Latina	16.8%	12.5%	11.4%
In central cities	45.8%	32.6%	19.7%
In rural areas	19.7%	18.7%	22.1%
More than 2 children under age 18	32.7%	13.3%	21.7%
Youngest child aged less than 6	65.9%	42.8%	49.9%
Never married	55.7%	29.3%	—
Average earnings	$1,516	$13,693	$12,631

Source: Calculated by authors from U.S. Bureau of the Census, Current Population Survey, March 1994.

amounts of paid labor without reliable childcare. Over half of the women receiving AFDC were never married. The great majority of nonrecipients were once married, giving them better prospects of collecting child support or alimony.

For comparison, the table includes married mothers. Married mothers showed still greater earning potential than single mothers receiving AFDC: they were more educated, older, and more likely to be white, non-Latina, and suburban. In short, the single mothers who resorted to AFDC did so because of a whole series of limitations on their earning opportunities—and the same is true for women on welfare today, post-AFDC.

Struggling to survive

The after-inflation value of welfare cash benefits has fallen since the early 1970s. So has the after-inflation average wage of non-supervisory workers. The wage loss has been most acute at the low end of the spectrum, where many single mothers are stuck: the minimum wage has lost one-quarter of its buying power since the mid-1970s.[25] It's been hard enough for *two*-parent families to survive; most of them have done so by jointly working more hours in a "family speed-up." How do single mothers survive?

Researchers who have spent years talking to low-income women offer an answer to this question: survival is hard. Women scrape through by piecing together a precarious patchwork of income from a variety of sources. They scrimp and go without things that many of us would consider necessities. And an unexpected expense—for example, a medical problem—or a delay in any income can precipitate a household financial crisis.

In 1991, sociologists Kathryn Edin and Laura Lein constructed average budgets based on multiple interviews with 450 low-income single mothers in Boston, Charleston, Chicago, and San Antonio.[26] As Table 5.3 shows, they found that these women were subsisting on extremely low incomes: $10,700 among welfare mothers and $14,900 among working single mothers—including Food Stamps and the Earned Income Credit, which supplements the income of very poor families.[27] While conservatives like to claim that welfare creates a cycle of dependency, the table clearly indicates that government aid (including AFDC and Supplemental Security Income grants as well as Food Stamps) cannot be relied on to cover even two-thirds of recipients' expenses. The inadequate levels of benefits force mothers to find alternative forms of income, even if some of these sources are not legal under welfare rules. Women do so in order to clothe, house, and feed their children.

Table 5.3 also graphically illustrates the limits of employment as a route out of poverty. Edin points out, "The presumption that a transition from welfare to work represents a move toward self-sufficiency or economic well-being ignores the fact that low-wage jobs neither pay enough to remove a family from poverty nor guarantee future access to better paying jobs."[28] Compared

Table 5.3 Scraping By

Average monthly income and expenses of AFDC recipients and
low-wage working single mothers in four cities (1991 dollars)

	Welfare mothers	Low-wage working mothers
Housing costs	$213	$341
Food costs	262	$249
Work-related costs		
Child care	7	66
Medical	18	56
Clothing	69	95
Transportation	31	57
Car payments and insurance	30	71
Other costs	245	308
TOTAL EXPENSES	$876	$1,243
Government assistance		
AFDC	307	—
Food Stamps	222	57
Supplemental Security Income	36	3
Earned Income Credit	3	25
Subtotal	$568	$85
Earnings		
Main (reported) job	19	777
Second job	—	59
Overtime	—	27
Income from unreported job	90	—
Income from underground economy	19	2
Contributions		
Family and friends	62	65
Boyfriends	56	60
Absent fathers	39	127
TOTAL INCOME	$892	$1,239

Note: Averages based on 214 AFDC recipients and 165 low-wage workers in Boston, Charleston, Chicago, and San Antonio.

Source: Kathryn J. Edin, "The Myths of Dependence and Self-Sufficiency: Women, Welfare, and Low-Wage Work," Focus (Madison, WI: Institute for Research on Poverty), vol. 17, no. 2 (fall/winter 1995): 1-9.

to women on AFDC, low-wage working mothers end up taking one step forward and two steps back. The average wage-earning mother in this group makes an additional $758 from her main job. But she loses $505 in government aid and takes on $190 in work-related expenses. What's more, on average, the wage-earning mothers pay $128 more per month on housing, because they have less access to housing subsidies. The bottom line is that a main job leaves these mothers $65 *behind* where they would have been on AFDC! It takes added earnings from a second job or overtime just to break even. Like AFDC mothers, low-wage working mothers cannot meet all of their families' needs with their own wages; they continue to depend on government aid (especially Food Stamps), and above all, on aid from family and friends. It's not surprising that while 86 percent of the AFDC recipients in this study planned to leave welfare for paid work at some point, 73 percent were deferring employment until they could lower the costs of work and improve their earning power.

While the family budget numbers are grim enough, welfare recipients' own descriptions of the difficulty of making ends meet are particularly poignant. Sociologist Mark Rank interviewed welfare recipients in Wisconsin during the 1980s, and their testimony is heartrending. "It's not just thinking about whether or not you can afford to go to a movie," commented one single mother of two, "but you have to think about can the kids and I stop and get a soda if we've been out running errands. It's a big decision, 'cause we just don't have much spending money."[29] Another woman, who had a car that was "about to rust out," talked about "having to choose between letting things go— in a situation that's unsafe—or destituting ourselves in order to fix it. Having to make that choice is really hard."[30] One woman who went on welfare after searching unsuccessfully for work for two years summed things up this way:

> This is probably about the lowest point in my life, and I hope I never reach it again. Because this is where you're just up against a wall. You can't make a move. You can't buy anything that you want for your home. You can't go on a vacation. You can't take a weekend off and go see things because it costs too much. And it's just such a waste of life.[31]

For most single mothers, economic survival is a constant struggle. This is true for those trying to support a family on meager welfare benefits and for women trapped in the low-wage labor market. Unfortunately, the ongoing process of welfare "reform" threatens to remove much of the limited support that does exist. In Chapter Six, we take a closer look at why U.S. policies have done so little to reduce poverty, and in Chapter Seven, we examine why many new policy proposals will do even less.

Notes

1. Roberta Spalter-Roth, Heidi Hartmann, and Linda Andrews, "Combining Work and Welfare," in *Sociology and the Public Agenda*, ed. William Julius Wilson (Newbury Park, CA: Sage Publications, 1993).
2. Computed by authors from U.S. Bureau of the Census, Current Population Survey, March 1994.
3. Jane Lewis, "Introduction," in *Women and Social Policies in Europe: Work, Family and the State*, ed. Jane Lewis (Aldershot, England: Edward Elgar, 1993), table 1.3.
4. Christopher Jencks, "Is the American Underclass Growing?" in *The Urban Underclass*, eds. Christopher Jencks and Paul E. Peterson (Washington, D.C.: Brookings Institution, 1991), table 15.
5. U.S. Department of Health and Human Services, *Vital Statistics of the United States, 1991, Volume I—Natality* (Hyattsville, MD: 1995), table 1-77.
6. U.S. Department of Commerce, *Statistical Abstract of the United States* (Washington, D.C.: Government Printing Office, 1994), table 80.
7. Demie Kurz, *For Richer, For Poorer: Women Confront Divorce* (London: Routledge, 1995).
8. Richard V. Burkhauser and Greg J. Duncan, "Economic Risks of Gender Roles: Income Loss and Life Events over the Life Course," *Social Science Quarterly*, vol. 70, no. 1 (March 1989). They define catastrophic income losses as ones involving a loss of 50 percent or more of a family's income-to-needs ratio (the ratio of the family's income to their poverty line).
9. Some research that suggests a link between male employment opportunities and marriage includes: William J. Wilson and Kathryn M. Neckerman, "Poverty and Family Structure: the Widening Gap Between Evidence and Public Policy Issues," in *Fighting Poverty: What Works and What Doesn't*, eds. Sheldon Danziger and Daniel Weinberg (Cambridge, MA: Harvard University Press, 1986); Sara McLanahan, Irwin Garfinkel, and Dorothy Watson, "Family Structure, Poverty, and

the Underclass," discussion paper 823-87, University of Wisconsin-Madison, Institute for Research on Poverty, 1987; Mark Testa, Nan Marie Astone, Marilyn Krogh, and Kathryn M. Neckerman, "Employment and Marriage among Inner-City Fathers," *Annals of the American Academy of Political and Social Science*, vol. 501 (January 1989).

10. Rebecca Blank, "What are the Trends in Nonmarital Births?" in *Looking Before We Leap: Social Science and Welfare Reform*, eds. R. Kent Weaver and William T. Dickens (Washington, D.C.: Brookings Institution, 1995).

11. Judith Stacey, "The New Family Values Crusaders," *The Nation* (25 July/1 August 1994): 119-21. See also Frank F. Furstenberg, Jr. and Andrew J. Cherlin, *Divided Families: What Happens to Children When Parents Part* (Cambridge, MA: Harvard University Press, 1991).

12. Sara S. McLanahan, "The Consequences of Single Motherhood," *The American Prospect* 18 (summer 1994).

13. Arline T. Geronimus and Sanders Korenman, "The Socioeconomic Consequences of Teen Childbearing Reconsidered," *Quarterly Journal of Economics* 107 (1992): pp. 1187-1214. See also Greg J. Duncan and Saul D. Hoffman, "Welfare Benefits, Economic Opportunities, and Out-of-Wedlock Births Among Black Teenage Girls," *Demography* 27, no. 4 (November 1990).

14. General Accounting Office, "Families on Welfare: Teenage Mothers Least Likely to Be Self-Sufficient" (Washington, D.C.: May 1994).

15. Center on Hunger, Poverty, and Nutrition Policy, "Statement on Key Welfare Reform Issues: The Empirical Evidence," Tufts University, Medford, MA, 1995.

16. Diana Pearce and Emily Knearl, "Teen Pregnancy, Welfare, and Poverty" (Washington, D.C.: Wider Opportunities for Women, 1994).

17. *Statistical Abstract of the United States,* op. cit., p. 858, table 1358.

18. Center on Hunger, Poverty, and Nutrition Policy, op. cit.

19. News release, University of Michigan, Research and Training Program on Poverty, the Underclass and Public Policy, School of Social Work, June 23, 1994.

20. Center on Budget and Policy Priorities, *Out of Wedlock Childbearing and Welfare Reform* (Washington, D.C.: 1995), and Jared Bernstein, "Welfare-Bashing Redux: The Return of Charles Murray," *The Humanist,* 55:1 (January/February 1995).

21. Blank, op. cit.

22. U.S. Bureau of the Census, *Studies in Household and Family Formation*, P-23, no. 179.

23. Institute for Women's Policy Research, "Measuring the Costs of Domestic Violence and the Cost Effectiveness of Interventions," report, Washington, D.C., May 31, 1995; Jody Raphael, "Domestic Violence: Telling the Untold Welfare-to-Work Story," Taylor Institute, Chicago, January 1995.

24. Arloc Sherman, *Wasting America's Future: The Children's Defense Fund Report on the Costs of Child Poverty* (Boston: Beacon Press, 1994).

25. William Spriggs and John Schmitt, "The Minimum Wage: Blocking the Low-wage Path," in *Reclaiming Prosperity,* eds. Todd Schafer and Jeff Faux (Armonk, NY: M.E. Sharpe, 1996).

26. Kathryn J. Edin and Laura Lein, *Making Ends Meet: How Single Mothers Survive Welfare and Low-Wage Work* (New York: Russell Sage Foundation, 1996).

27. Kathryn J. Edin, "The Myths of Dependence and Self-Sufficiency: Women, Welfare, and Low-Wage Work," *Focus* (Madison, WI: Institute for Research on Poverty), vol. 17, no. 2 (fall/winter 1995).

28. Ibid., pp. 1-2.

29. Mark R. Rank, *Living on the Edge: The Realities of Welfare in America* (New York: Columbia University Press, 1994), p. 61.

30. Ibid., p. 57.

31. Ibid., p. 52.

6

What's Wrong With Current Poverty Policies?

The anti-poverty policies of the United States do not work very well. The clearest evidence of their ineffectiveness is that poverty has persisted at relatively high levels and has even grown during some periods over the last couple of decades. Does this mean that government action cannot end economic deprivation, or that anti-poverty policies have actually contributed to the growth of poverty? Not at all. But our efforts have been incomplete and halfhearted, guided by flawed theories. So it should not surprise us that we have failed to tackle poverty.

A weak track record: The United States compared to other countries

Comparison with other industrialized countries helps to place the U.S. anti-poverty track record in perspective. In contrast to these other nations, the United States has been remarkably unsuccessful in lifting families—especially single-mother families—out of poverty. Researchers have found that in the late 1980s, not only did the United States have a higher poverty rate for nonelder families (those headed by someone under sixty-five) than six other industrialized countries, it also had the most ineffective tax and transfer system when it came to pulling those families out of poverty.[1] To make international comparisons, the researchers defined a family as poor if its size-adjusted income

Figure 6.1 United States Has Highest Percentage of Poor Families

Percentage of poor among nonelder families in seven industrialized countries, various years

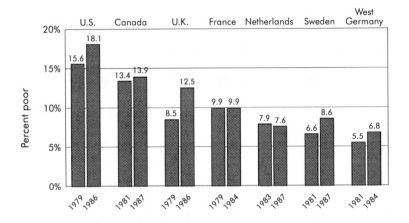

Note: The poverty income threshold is equal to 50 percent of the national median income. Includes only households with heads twenty to fifty-five years old in each country. Data come from the Luxembourg Income Study, and poverty calculations for countries above have not been updated since the mid-1980s.

Source: Joint Center for Political and Economic Studies, *Poverty, Inequality and the Crisis of Social Policy*, September 1991.

was 50 percent or less of the national median income among families with heads aged twenty to fifty-five. Figure 6.1 depicts the poverty rates for families with heads in this age range for the United States, Canada, the United Kingdom, the former West Germany, the Netherlands, France, and Sweden in years near 1980 and in the mid-1980s. Figure 6.2 shows the percentage of nonelder families lifted out of poverty by the combination of transfer and tax policies in the same seven nations. It asks the question: Of families who would have been poor *before* receiving government cash aid and paying taxes, what percentage were no longer poor *after* transfers and taxes were applied?

Of the countries studied, the United States had the highest

Figure 6.2   United States Policies Least Effective in Alleviating Poverty   *Percentage of poor, nonelder families that were lifted out of poverty as a result of tax and transfer policies in seven industrialized countries, various years*

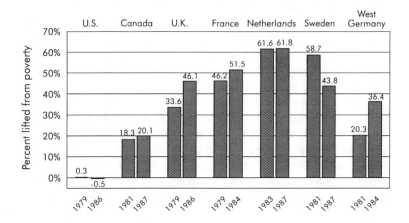

Note: The poverty income threshold is equal to 50 percent of the national median income. Includes only households with heads twenty to fifty-five years old in each country. Data come from the Luxembourg Income Study, and poverty calculations for countries above have not been updated since the mid-1980s.

Source: Joint Center for Political and Economic Studies, *Poverty, Inequality and the Crisis of Social Policy,* September 1991.

poverty rates—about two to three times those of France, the Netherlands, Sweden, and West Germany. Figure 6.2 helps explain why: U.S. tax and transfer policies had the worst record of lifting families out of poverty. Whereas most countries' policies boosted about half of the at-risk families out of poverty, embarrassingly, U.S. tax and transfer programs actually made families *poorer* in 1986: taxes pushed more into poverty than transfers pulled out. Since then, some tax policies have changed—most important, the Earned Income Credit has considerably reduced the taxation of working-poor families. Meanwhile, transfers for poor, nonelder families have actually fallen when adjusted for inflation.

Whom U.S. policies help most

The story remains the same when we switch from the researchers' internationally comparable definition of poverty back to the familiar U.S. definition of the poverty line. The U.S. poverty line for a family of four in 1993 was $14,800—less than half of the median income of all families headed by persons aged twenty to fifty-five, which stood at $30,900. But even given this lower poverty threshold (and leaving aside the impact of taxation), government transfers boosted less than half of all at-risk families out of poverty (Table 6.1).

What's more, some family types benefit significantly more from government income transfer programs than others, as Table 6.1 reveals. Social Security, because it is universal and relatively generous, has been quite successful in staving off poverty among elders. It lifted three out of every four pretransfer-poor elder families from poverty—a success rate to be proud of. Interestingly, government cash transfers also work relatively well for

Table 6.1   The Helping Hand Is Unsteady

Percentage of U.S. families pulled out of poverty by government income transfers, 1993

Type of family	Before transfer poverty rate	After transfer poverty rate	Percent of pre-transfer poor pulled out of poverty by government transfers
Two-adult with children	14%	11%	24%
Two-adult without children (under 65)	9	5	47
Single mother	58	52	11
Single father	28	24	15
Lone male (under 65)	23	18	21
Lone female (under 65)	30	25	18
Head over 65 (no children)	57	15	75
All families	28	16	42

Source: Calculated by authors from U.S. Bureau of the Census, Current Population Survey, March 1994.

two-adult families without children, even though they have the lowest poverty rate.

On the other hand, government transfers are least effective for female-headed families, lifting one in six lone females and one in nine single-mother families out of poverty. In short, government transfer policies do not particularly help nonelder women who do not live with other adult family members (typically men)—despite the fact that these families are much more likely to be poor. It is hard to avoid the gender implications: current government transfer policies keep nonelder women without men poorer than other family types.

Government aid also has an uneven impact on families of different racial and ethnic groups who would have fallen below the poverty line without government cash assistance. Those boosted out of poverty include:

- 51 percent of families headed by a white, non-Latino person;
- 25 percent of black families;
- 21 percent of Latino families;
- 21 percent of Asian families;
- 35 percent of Native-American families;
- and only 7 percent of black single-mother families—about one in fourteen!

In short, government transfers help white families more than families of color—and single-mother families least of all.

Why does government aid do so much less to alleviate poverty among single mothers than among elders? Is it because many more single mothers need help? Evidently not: as Table 6.1 shows, equal percentages of single mothers and elders would live in poverty without government transfers. In absolute numbers, in fact, three times as many elders as single mothers would be poor without that aid. What *does* make a difference is that the government offers far more generous assistance to elders. In 1993, the average public assistance (including AFDC) received by single mothers at all income levels was $1,418, while the average Social Security payment for families headed by someone over the age of sixty-five was $9,081. If we limit our attention to families that would have been poor without government aid, the average payments shift to $2,389 for single mothers and $8,478

Figure 6.3 Single Parents Fare Better in Other Countries

Percentage of poor single-parent families before and after tax and transfer policies in seven industrialized countries, various years

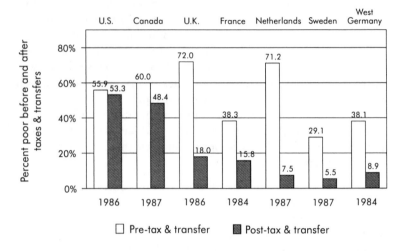

Note: Poverty line is defined as the median income of nonelder families.

Source: Katherine McFate, Timothy Smeeding, and Lee Rainwater, "Markets and States; Poverty Trends and Transfer Effectiveness in the 1980s," tables 1.8 and 1.10, in *Poverty, Inequality and the Future of Social Policy: Western States in the New World Order*, eds. Katherine McFate, Roger Lawson, and William Julius Wilson (New York: Russell Sage, 1995), pp. 29–66.

for elders. Once again, we see a double standard where women and their children are concerned.

Cross-national comparison shows that the gap between the United States and other countries yawns widest when it comes to single-parent poverty. As Figure 6.3 shows, single-parent households in the United States were far more likely to be poor than their counterparts in other countries in the late 1980s (using the internationally comparable definition of poverty described earlier). The contrast with Sweden is astonishing: U.S. single parents had a poverty rate ten times as high as Swedish single-parent families. In some cases—France and Sweden—part of the reason is that other countries' labor markets are more hospitable to single parents, but in *every* case, other countries' more generous transfer programs account for most of the difference.

And the United States' lead in single-parent poverty is growing, even compared to the economy most similar to ours—Canada, our neighbor to the north. Economists Maria Hanratty and Rebecca Blank applied U.S. poverty line definitions to Canada (remember that this line is different from the international poverty standard). In both countries, they counted government noncash transfers (except medical assistance) as income, and looked only at families with heads aged eighteen to sixty. They discovered that between 1979 and 1986:

- Among two-adult families with no children, the United States started out in 1979 with a slightly lower poverty rate than Canada and ended up in 1986 with the same poverty rate.
- U.S. two-adult families *with* children fared somewhat worse. They began with a poverty rate a bit lower than their Canadian counterparts, but by 1986, had climbed to a poverty rate two percentage points higher.
- U.S. single-parent families, whose poverty rate started two percentage points above that of Canadian single parents at the outset of the seven-year period, shot up to a poverty rate *fifteen percentage points* above that of the Canadians!

Hanratty and Blank found that economic and demographic change could not explain the divergence between U.S. and Canadian poverty rates. Instead, over the 1980s, Canadian welfare policies became more generous while U.S. policies became stingier—especially where single mothers were concerned.[2]

Noncash benefits and welfare for the well-off

Conservatives are quick to point out that since the federal and state governments also dispense noncash benefits, such as Food Stamps and housing subsidies, the plight of the poor is not as severe as cash income alone would suggest. So let's take a closer look at noncash benefits to see how much difference they make. It turns out that factoring in such benefits makes little difference in poverty rates (as Hanratty and Blank confirmed). What's more, nonpoor families receive these benefits, too. And employers also provide noncash benefits, such as pensions and health insurance. Once we take employer-provided health insurance into account, single-mother families fall behind elder and two-parent families in total noncash benefits. And if the goal is a complete accounting for government assistance, we must also consider government "welfare" programs aiding middle-class and even wealthy families and businesses—which eclipse welfare for the poor in terms of dollar amounts.

Let's start with some basic facts. The government provides a variety of noncash benefits, which are largely "means tested"—that is, eligibility is tied to income. Forty-six percent of all families in the United States in 1993 benefited from these noncash programs, including Food Stamps, housing assistance, Medicaid, Medicare, and school lunches. And these programs are not just for the poor: while 56 percent of poor families received at least one of these benefits, so did 40 percent of families who were not poor. The Census Bureau assigns a cash value to these benefits, and in 1993, the average family received benefits worth $1,300. Families with a head older than sixty-five received the highest average amount of government noncash transfers, valued at $3,878, followed by single-mother families with an average of $1,726.3

Adding the cash value of the benefits to a family's income would push many families above the poverty line. Yet some of the benefits—notably health care—are only available when a family needs them and cannot be used to purchase anything else. Including the cash value of health benefits in calculating poverty and well-being would mean that between two families with equivalent income and other forms of nonincome benefits, the one with the perennially sick child would be considered "better off." Suppose, instead, that we only count as income the cash value of Food Stamps, housing assistance, and school lunches. This would indeed reduce poverty, but not by much —from 16 to 15 percent. For single-mother families, counting nonincome benefits reduces the poverty rate from 52 to 48 percent. In short, even including the cash value of Food Stamps, housing assistance, and school lunches, single mothers still face an unbearably high likelihood of being poor.

The government is not the only provider of noncash benefits. Employers provide them as well. The two largest benefits provided by employers are pensions and health insurance contributions—both of which are more likely to go to higher-paid employees and neither of which counts toward family income. The Census Bureau does not place a cash value on employer pension contributions, but it has recently begun to estimate the value of employer contributions to health insurance. In 1993, the average amount families received in the form of health insurance was $1,625, but this varied considerably by family type. Among nonelder family types, two adults with children received the highest average benefit, at $2,748 per year, while single-mother families on average got the least, only $878. Just under half of all families (48 percent) received some nonincome benefits in the form of employer-sponsored health insurance.

Figure 6.4 depicts the dollar amount of nonincome benefits received by families. As with income transfers, elder families receive the most government nonincome benefits. When employer-provided health coverage is included, elders still receive the highest total in noncash aid, followed closely by two-adult families. Single mothers and single individuals, however, lag behind.

In addition to noncash benefits, many of this country's wealthy receive "invisible" welfare payments in the form of tax breaks. For example, home mortgage interest is deductible up to a dazzling $1 million per year. Lowering this ceiling to $250,000 would only affect the wealthiest 5 percent of Americans, but would save taxpayers $10 billion a year.[4]

U.S. government assistance does not all go to individuals and families—much of it goes to corporations. In fact, the $22 billion spent on AFDC in 1992 is far outshadowed by corporate welfare, which amounts to $86 billion annually in federal subsidies and an equal amount in tax breaks, according to a 1995 estimate.[5] Accelerated depreciation (which allows companies to depreciate the value of plant and equipment much faster than it wears out, for tax purposes) alone costs the government $32 billion a year.[6] And that's just the *federal* government. State and local governments frequently offer tax breaks and subsidies to attract businesses, sometimes spending literally hundreds of thousands of dollars per job to attract a large plant.

Figure 6.4 Who Gets In-Kind Benefits

Average government-provided and employer-provided nonincome benefits by family type, 1993

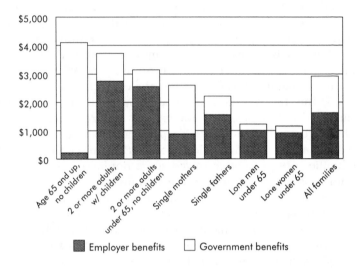

Employer benefits ☐ Government benefits

Note: Employer benefits include the value of employer's contribution to health insurance. Government benefits include the value of Food Stamps, housing assistance, school lunches, Medicaid, and Medicare.

Source: Calculated by authors from U.S. Bureau of the Census, Current Population Survey, March 1994.

To curb federal corporate welfare, the Washington-based Progressive Policy Institute recommends $48 billion in annual cuts.[7] This is not to say that the government should never provide aid to business. When such aid significantly boosts the nation's productivity, and particularly when the benefits are spread broadly to workers and consumers, there is often a case to be made for assistance. The point is that the same case can be made for aid to struggling families, especially those raising the children who constitute this country's future. And while corporate welfare currently spills well beyond the point where it genuinely represents a sound investment in the nation's productivity, the same generosity has not been applied to aid poor families.

Flawed policies, flawed theories of poverty

Why does the United States have such a bad track record on alleviating poverty? And why has anti-poverty policy shortchanged mothers in particular? Dating back to their origins, U.S. poverty policies have always been limited in scope, stigmatized the poor, and incorporated gender and race biases. Over the last thirty years, the political pendulum has swung from liberal to conservative, and the theories guiding anti-poverty policy have changed. Yet consistent flaws in these theories have always hobbled the government's effectiveness in lifting families up and out of poverty.

A long history of stinginess

British settlers in what became the United States began institutionalizing relief programs shortly after their arrival in North America, establishing the first such program in the Plymouth Colony in 1642.[8] Relief programs modeled on the British poor laws were in effect through the 19th century. They rested on local funding and administration, and distinguished sharply between the "deserving" and "undeserving" poor. Importantly, local governments sought to make welfare undesirable by providing benefits well below prevailing wage levels, attaching degrading conditions, and requiring work in many cases. The overseers of the poor in Beverly, Massachusetts, expressed a typical view in the early 1800s: they worried that the "industrious poor" would be "discouraged by observing that bounty bestowed upon the idle, which they can only obtain by the sweat of their brow."[9]

The outright degradation of relief recipients was greatest during the colonial era. Some colonies required recipients to wear a badge bearing the letter "P" for "pauper"; others denied recipients the right to marry or made them subject to jail, slavery, or indenture. Some restrictions persisted for decades. In the 1930s, for instance, fourteen states still banned welfare recipients from voting or holding political office.

Beginning in the 1700s, relief authorities often imposed work requirements, setting up workhouses or, in some cases, "houses of industry" that provided private-sector jobs at rock-bottom wages. In the 1800s, the authorities gravitated toward more punitive work regimes, requiring hard physical labor that some-times amounted to make-work.

While stigmas and restrictions were the norm for white, na-tive-born poor people, in many instances people of color and immigrants were excluded from assistance altogether. African-American slaves, of course, were at the mercy of their masters. For decades after Emancipation, local welfare authorities simply classified blacks and other people of color as "undeserving," forestalling any welfare assistance. Even the welfare rights move-ment of the late 1960s discovered continuing barriers to the eli-gibility of women of color. Native Americans have had a particu-larly bitter history. After hundreds of years of being forcibly pushed from their lands and livelihoods, they were repeatedly promised federal assistance in 19th-century treaties, only to have these promises, like many others, broken. Though federal assis-tance reaches Native-American reservations today, they remain the poorest areas in the country; in some, such as the Wine-mucca Colony in Nevada, *all* members are poor.[10]

In addition to racial distinctions, welfare policies from early on embodied what sociologist Mimi Abramovitz calls the "work ethic" and the "family ethic."[11] The work ethic insists that relief must pay less than wage labor, in order to avoid disrupting low-wage labor markets. The family ethic holds that a woman should marry a man capable of supporting her, and that assistance should reward women who conform to this ethic (such as wid-ows) and punish those who do not (such as divorced or never-married mothers). Based on the family ethic, relief for men and women typically differed. At the turn of the 20th century, for example, Progressive Era welfare programs built in gender dis-tinctions, offering Workmen's Compensation for industrial working-class men and Mother's Aid for impoverished widows with children. Both programs were also limited primarily to whites.

The Feds step in

The watershed 1935 Social Security Act created a national system of relief. What made this effort different from previous ones was the full recognition that the capitalist system couldn't always provide a job for male breadwinners or assure economic viability for families without a man. But, as with the state and local efforts that preceded it, the work and family ethics lay at the core of the legislation. For "deserving" workers unemployed through no fault of their own, the act offered Unemployment Insurance. For those families without a viable male breadwinner, two distinct programs were established. The first, Old Age, Survivor, and Disability Insurance (OASDI, Social Security's official name), gave support to the elderly according to their lifetime earnings, and in 1939, also supported the widows and children of men who had logged substantial earnings. The second, Aid to Dependent Families (later to become Aid to Families with Dependent Children), was a residual program, offering low levels of aid to those mothers (mainly widows, initially) for whom OASDI did not adequately provide. The law locked in distinctions between "men's" and "women's" welfare programs, and between "deserving" and "undeserving" recipients.

The color line also persisted. Due to the influence of southern congressmen, the Social Security Act perpetuated a racial double standard. The act's core programs, unemployment compensation and old-age assistance, excluded agricultural workers and domestic servants, and thus the majority of black workers in the South. Blacks were left to less generous social assistance programs. Moreover, southerners purged from the legislation any hint of uniform national standards. In practice, the state and local authorities who administered social welfare programs gave African Americans second-class treatment.[12]

In some form, all of these double standards remain with us to this day. In the United States, anti-poverty policies continue to revolve around the firm beliefs that hard work pays off, traditional "family values" should be rewarded, and people of color relying on welfare are less deserving than other recipients. Nonetheless, policy emphases have shifted over time. Policymakers in the 1960s stressed the need to assure economic growth in order to reduce poverty. A robust economy, they argued, would reduce unemployment; as more people had jobs, poverty would decline.[13] These liberal policies are often called Keynesian, in honor of British economist John Maynard Keynes, who in the 1930s developed theories about how governments could stimulate economic expansion. The Keynesian approach focused not on the characteristics of individuals and families who were poor, but rather on the economic environment conditioning poor people's opportunities.

In the late 1970s, a much more conservative theory rapidly supplanted Keynesian economics. The emphasis on jobs still held sway—but instead of focusing on the structural problems of the economy, policymakers insisted that structural problems of individuals and families caused poverty. Human capital—such individual characteristics as education level and job experience—and motivation, rather than the unemployment rate, were seen as the determining factors in one's ability to get and keep a job.[14] Since the early 1980s, changes in anti-poverty programs have put the spotlight on single mothers, and the main thrust of the programs has been toward job training and placement plus behavioral restrictions, attempts to bolster the same old work and family ethics.

Despite their contrasting perspectives, both the economic growth-based and behavior-based approaches to alleviating poverty are flawed and fail to address widespread poverty among single-mother families. Let's take a closer look at each approach.

The growth theory: A rising tide lifts all boats

When the Johnson administration began its "War on Poverty" in the mid-1960s, the conventional wisdom held that policies promoting economic growth were the most effective way to combat poverty. Further economic growth was also assumed to be the best way to promote a higher standard of living for all and bring about greater economic equality.

During the 1960s and 1970s, the emphasis on growth played out both in attempts to stimulate the national economy, and in targeted aid to depressed regions (such as Appalachia) and localities. The geography-based regional and local job-creation programs included rural literacy and development projects, job training, urban development, and education grants. To some extent, the notion that a rising tide lifts all boats persists among many policymakers at the state and national levels, but it has more recently been translated into new policy prescriptions. The "trickle-down" economic policies of eliminating regulations on businesses while decreasing taxation on corporations and

Figure 6.5   Shifting Fortunes

Percentage of income received by richest 5 percent and poorest 40 percent of families in the United States, 1947–1994

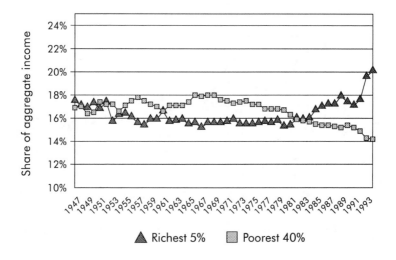

▲ Richest 5%   ▨ Poorest 40%

Source: U.S. Bureau of the Census, *Current Population Reports*, 1988, 1989, 1991, and 1992. Data for 1993 and 1994 come from Center on Budget and Policy Priorities, *Poverty and Income Trends: 1994*, p. 53.

wealthy individuals represent a conservative variation on the "rising tide" approach.

The central proposition of the rising tide approach is that a growing economy will mean more jobs and more income for all. And indeed, in the 1960s and the early 1970s, nationwide growth did lessen poverty and increase equality. Since the early 1970s, however, the links between economic growth, reduced poverty, and greater equality have become much weaker. Despite economic growth, inequality among families in the United States has increased considerably, and growth has done little to reduce poverty. Figure 6.5 depicts the shifting distribution of income by comparing the richest 5 percent of the population to the poorest 40 percent: while the bottom 40 percent made gains during the 1960s, the top 5 percent pulled ahead once more over the 1970s

Figure 6.6   Back to the Future?

Poverty rates of persons under eighteen, persons eighteen to sixty-four, and persons sixty-five and older in the United States, 1959–1995

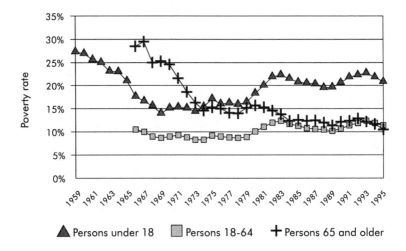

▲ Persons under 18   ▨ Persons 18-64   ✚ Persons 65 and older

Note: Data for persons eighteen to sixty-four and sixty-five and older not available before 1966.

Source: U.S. Bureau of the Census, *Poverty in the United States: 1995*, P60-194, 1996.

and 1980s. Figure 6.6 shows the poverty rate from 1959 to 1995 in the United States for three age groups: people under eighteen, people eighteen to sixty-four, and people sixty-five years and older. Despite ups and downs reflecting short-term booms and busts in the economy, the long-term downward trend in poverty rates ended in the 1970s, and poverty rates among children have risen markedly since that time. This reversal took place even though long-term economic growth continued (with occasional setbacks when recessions hit).

There are several reasons for this seeming paradox of economic growth accompanied by increased inequality and persistent poverty. First, the fruits of that growth have not been equally shared. Between 1983 and 1989, close to 40 percent of the increase in income and 66 percent of the increase in financial wealth went to the richest 1 percent of the population.[15] Further, income growth in the 1980s was due, in large part, to property income gains, not increases in wage income. The high interest rates of the 1980s, the fortunes made in leveraged buyouts and corporate mergers, and the real-estate speculation bonanza all largely benefited those with lots of money to begin with. Meanwhile, the decline in manufacturing jobs in the United States lowered the standard of living for many workers—especially men without college degrees. Average wages for non-supervisory workers fell (after adjusting for inflation), meaning that for a growing number of families, jobs do not provide an escape from poverty. The growth-based approach of poverty policy in the post-World War II period assumed growing industrial employment for breadwinners. That assumption no longer holds.

Massachusetts provides a good case study of the changing relationship among growth, poverty, and inequality. The rising tide of wage growth in Massachusetts in the 1980s—the "Massachusetts miracle"—was among the most spectacular of all the states. Yet the "miracle" was not enough to lift many families out of poverty. Massachusetts saw average incomes rise rapidly from 1979 to 1987, with a 16.5 percent increase in the average inflation-adjusted family income (compared to 4.2 percent for the whole United States). But not all families "cashed in." While two-adult families without children saw their incomes rise by 36 percent, two-adult families with children only experienced a 14 percent increase—less than the state average. Faring the worst of all, however, were single-mother families—the family type most likely to be poor at the onset of the miraculous economic performance. Single-mother families' incomes grew by a puny 2 percent, while their poverty rate went from 48 percent in 1979 to 47 percent in 1987.[16] In the United States as a whole, the income rise was not as dramatic, but the same pattern prevailed: single mothers got almost no advantage from economic growth.

In short, an economic recovery *on its own* offers little hope of economic relief for single-mother families. Even before the Massachusetts experience, conservatives seized on this fact and drew a simple conclusion: it must be the fault of the single mothers themselves.

Blaming the victim: Single-mother bashing

Government-sponsored poverty programs of the 1980s focused on regulating the behavior of single mothers. This represented a shift away from the earlier model that used government spending to propel national growth while assisting rural and urban areas with high levels of poverty. Beginning in the late 1970s, these programs were sharply curtailed as federal, state, and local government deficits put increased pressure on officials to reduce social welfare spending. In 1981, the Reagan administration turned fifty programs into nine block grants, reducing their funding by 12 percent.[17]

At the same time, the Reagan administration severely tightened eligibility requirements for nonelder individuals receiving income transfers, specifically AFDC and disability-based SSI payments. And for those still receiving welfare, the 1988 Family Support Act made job placement a paramount goal. Reagan administration spokespeople claimed that welfare created dependency and that government did more harm than good by offering "handouts." Despite the fact that the government offers all sorts of "handouts" to disabled veterans, unemployed people, and elders, welfare recipients were painted with a broad brushstroke as weak and dependent for having to rely on government income as a main source of support. Racial stereotyping helped fuel this assault, despite the fact that most welfare recipients are white and non-Latino (other government assistance programs go even more overwhelmingly to whites).

The demonization of the poor, especially welfare recipients, has reached new heights in the 1990s. Political candidates (Democrat and Republican alike), talk show hosts, and conservative journalists use welfare as a political football. The range of rhetoric spans from President Clinton's popular 1992 campaign promise to "end welfare as we know it" to Rush Limbaugh's blast, "The poor in this country are the biggest piglets at the mother pig and her nipples."[18] A heightened frequency of racist salvos directed at immigrants and people of color has fed these attacks on welfare. In a short period of time, we have seen the 1960s' War on Poverty evolve into a war on the poor.

Conservatives have particularly focused on out-of-wedlock births in an attempt to pump up the family ethic in welfare reform at a time when family structure is in tremendous flux. The two pillars that have allowed for an extremely limited social safety net in the United States are crumbling: plentiful industrial-based jobs for male breadwinners and the traditional married-couple family. The increasing diversity of families, along with the inability of the growing economy to alleviate the pangs of poverty, has created a new conundrum for policymakers. Unfortunately, far too many have responded by lashing out at the victims of economic inequality.

Charles Murray and Robert Rector, the self-styled bad boys of poverty research

Well-funded conservative think tanks have played a major role in fueling the poverty policy shifts of the 1980s and 1990s. True, the "single-mother-bashing" approach to poverty policy is driven primarily by ideology, not by logical arguments. But there are researchers who devote themselves to providing a "scientific" gloss to this punitive philosophy. Foremost among them are sociologist Charles Murray of the American Enterprise Institute (AEI) and Robert Rector of the Heritage Foundation. The clout wielded by AEI and Heritage, two of the leading Washington-based right-wing think tanks, can hardly be overstated. These two conservative brain trusts, along with others, have saturated the media and Congress for years with their calls for dismantling AFDC and adopting what they call a "tough love" approach to poor people.[19] In the first 100 days of the 1995 Congress, staff members from the Heritage Foundation testified before lawmakers forty times.[20]

Lurking behind the soundbites is the dubious scholarship of Murray and Rector. These two delight in appearing controversial and present themselves as courageous scholars who dare to say what others won't. But in reality, how much courage is involved in riding a swelling conservative tide? Murray and Rector are simply providing intellectual cover for views that blame poor people and "big government" for perpetuating poverty, and they have become wealthy right-wing celebrities as a result.

Murray's notoriety began with the publication of his book *Losing Ground* in 1984.[21] The centerpiece of the book was a chart that showed U.S. poverty rates rising through the 1970s and early 1980s, at a time when government spending on poverty was also rising. Murray glibly concluded that government anti-poverty programs were *contributing* to poverty by making it easier to survive without working for pay. He argued that government policies should instead make poverty as uncomfortable as possible—in his view, the squalid workhouses of old were a reasonable solution.

Critics pointed out that Murray had overlooked some of the obvious explanations for the increases on his chart. First, Murray choose to ignore the fact that long struggles to distribute benefits to those who were legally entitled but effectively excluded from receiving welfare were finally being won. Some of the spending expansion in the late 1960s and 1970s was directly attributable to successful lawsuits challenging restrictive eligibility rules, along with the organizing done by those in the civil rights and welfare rights movements. These efforts transformed what had been a small program largely restricted to white widows into a welfare program increasingly available to single and nonwhite parents as well. Second, through the 1970s and early 1980s, a harsher economic climate pushed more people into poverty, which in turn led to more spending on the entitlement programs available to poor people. Economists have demonstrated that the poverty rate closely tracks overall economic well-being and rose consistently in step with economic deterioration over the 1970s and 1980s.[22] In fact, although after-inflation AFDC benefit levels and coverage rates (AFDC recipiency as a percentage of the poor) rose in the late 1960s and early 1970s, benefits and coverage *fell* from the mid-1970s onward—so Murray's claim of growing government generosity rings hollow.

But Murray brushed these objections aside, and was off and running. In 1994 he made headlines again, along with coauthor Richard Herrnstein, with the publication of *The Bell Curve*.[23] Herrnstein and Murray declared that income differences—including those of race—are primarily and increasingly a result of genetically determined intelligence. Again, the evidence for this far-reaching claim is flimsy indeed, as numerous critics have pointed out.[24] Leaving aside problems of sloppy statistical methods (which are rife in *The Bell Curve*), there are several reasons for rejecting this claim. First, many differences in intelligence test scores are due to systematic differences in home, school, and neighborhood environments—differences that, like genes, tend to be passed down from parent to child in our stratified society.

Second, performance on standardized tests is affected by the expectations of oneself and others. For example, in a study on black and white Stanford University undergraduates, psychologists Claude Steele and Joshua Aronson found that blacks performed worse than whites when required to identify their race at the start of the test, but performed better than whites when this requirement was removed.[25]

Third, race and gender discrimination in employment are alive and well. Recent "audit" studies that sent black and white applicants with identical résumés to apply for jobs found that, on average, whites were more likely than blacks to get called in for an interview, and more likely to be offered a job if interviewed.[26] Direct interviews with employers reveal that many of them freely voice crude racial stereotypes.[27] And sex segregation in jobs, along with the accompanying gender stereotypes, persists despite women's limited inroads into "men's" work.[28]

In other recent broadsides, Murray has argued that rising welfare benefits have driven increases in single motherhood.[29] Again, this position is difficult to maintain, since even his own charts show that the most dramatic rises in single motherhood have taken place during times when inflation-adjusted AFDC benefits decreased. But as always, the facts have not slowed Murray down.

Rector echoes Murray's views, contending that "welfare is an insidious system in which the more you spend, the more clientele for the programs you create. . . . The more you spend, the more you erode the work ethic, the more out-of-wedlock births you have." Unlike Murray, Rector doesn't write books and has stayed out of academic debates. But his impact on policy is even greater than Murray's. As a policy analyst for the Heritage Foundation, he has been directly involved in lobbying Congress, providing intellectual fodder for conservative groups, and drafting legislation. "He's the think-tanker for a large network of people," comments Stuart Butler, Heritage's director of domestic policy studies.[30] Rector is pushing a harsh welfare reform agenda that has increasingly found a home in state and federal legislation: cuts in benefit levels, strict work requirements, and making benefits contingent upon "responsible behavior" (for example, requiring teen mothers to live with their parents).[31]

Appendix B of this book, a table of myths and facts compiled by economist Dorothy Seavey, provides a concise and well-documented counterpoint to much of the misinformation and myths generated by the Murrays and Rectors of the world.

Spending on welfare: Not too much, but too little

> In 1992, federal, state and local governments spent $305 billion on means-tested welfare programs for low-income Americans. Welfare now absorbs 5% of the Gross National Product, up from 1.5% in 1965 when the War on Poverty began.
>
> —*Heritage Foundation*[32]

This soundbite exemplifies the Heritage Foundation's myth-making machine at work. But a closer look at Heritage's numbers is instructive. There has been an enormous amount of media attention devoted to AFDC and its successor program, Temporary Assistance to Needy Families (TANF). Both programs, however, have represented a tiny—and recently shrinking—portion of the government budget.

As a percent of both the Gross Domestic Product (GDP) and the federal budget, combined federal spending on AFDC and Food Stamps has declined. In 1980, the two programs accounted for 0.8 percent of the GDP and 3.2 percent of the federal budget. By 1993, the two programs made up 0.7 percent of the GDP and 2.4 percent of the federal budget.[33] With federal spending on TANF now capped at $16.4 billion per year, these percentages stand to diminish still further. State spending on AFDC has also remained low. In 1970, states spent 3 percent of their budgets on AFDC benefits; by 1993, that percentage dropped to just under 2 percent.[34] And TANF frees states to spend still less on welfare.

Because of rising health care costs, a much larger percentage of state and federal budgets goes toward Medicaid. In 1992, Medicaid took up 5 percent of the federal budget, up from 2.5 percent in 1980.[35] It is only by including Medicaid as "welfare spending" that the figures used by the Heritage Foundation resemble reality. But less than 30 percent of total Medicaid spending is for welfare recipients.[36] The lion's share of Medicaid goes to elders and others who need long-term care; middle-class families rely on Medicaid to pay for their ailing parents in nursing homes. The rapidly rising cost of health care—whether publicly or privately financed—cannot and should not be blamed on the health care demands of poor children and their mothers.

And what about the $305 billion figure? Government spending on poor women and their children is one-quarter of the Heritage Foundation's purported figure. In 1992, federal and state governments spent a combined total of $43 billion on AFDC and Food Stamps. Total Medicaid spending for families receiving AFDC was $27.5 billion. So an accurate estimate of the costs of welfare spending in that year is $70.5 billion. By way of comparison, federal spending on two common middle-class tax exemptions came in at just under $100 billion: the value of the tax exemption for employer-sponsored health insurance was $47 billion and the mortgage deduction from income taxes was $49 billion.[37]

The Heritage Foundation's depiction of a bloated welfare state is a myth, yet the crisis of U.S. anti-poverty policy is a real one. The move away from economic development strategies to an individually based anti-poverty program focused on pushing poor people into jobs has not worked for single mothers and their children. It has failed to reduce poverty among single-mother families, and it has failed to make women less "dependent." Poverty rates among children and single-mother families have steadily risen, and the rates at which low-income single mothers return to welfare after getting off have not improved. The failure to reduce poverty among single-mother families, however, is not due to the failures of the recipients or the excessive generosity of the welfare payments. Rather, this failure results from the inadequacy of poverty programs, the inability of the labor market to adequately absorb and compensate women workers with limited education, and the fragility of traditional family relations.

Specifically, welfare grants pay not too much, but too little. Since AFDC payments did not automatically rise with inflation and states have been reluctant to increase payments, welfare has taken fewer and fewer single mothers out of poverty. In 1973, 22 percent of all single-mother families were lifted out of poverty by government assistance, but only 11 percent were in 1993.[38] AFDC benefits for a family of three in a typical state fell from $690 in 1970 to $366 in 1994 (using 1994 dollars).[39] Nationwide, *fewer* poor children receive AFDC today than in past decades. The percentage of poor children receiving AFDC peaked in 1973 at 80 percent, but had dropped to 59 percent by 1990.[40]

Eligibility requirements restrict welfare to a small number of very needy families. To be eligible to receive cash assistance, one must be extremely poor and have children (or be pregnant). Income eligibility varies from state to state and by length of time on welfare. Federal requirements stipulated that individuals might only own a car with a net market value of $1,500 or less, and might have no more than $1,000 in cash, checking and savings accounts, or other assets. Once on welfare, families were legally allowed to keep $50 of any child support payments per month, remitting the rest to the state. Under new federal legislation, states have complete discretion over these requirements, for good or ill.

Welfare is funded jointly by the federal government and states. The total amount of money, adjusted for inflation, spent by states and the federal government on AFDC in the mid-1990s was no higher than it was in the early 1970s. And while total spending for the Food Stamp program has increased over the same period, it has not been able to keep up with the increase in the numbers of poor women and children. Between 1971 and 1993, the number of poor people in female-headed families increased by 100 percent, but the number of AFDC recipients only increased by 50 percent.[41]

The notion that the United States spends too much on welfare is strained indeed. U.S. relief programs started out stingy and, for the most part, have remained so for over 300 years. Guided by the "work ethic," the "family ethic," and durable racial stereotypes, the federal, state, and local governments have kept benefits low, tied them to work and family structure requirements, and excluded whole groups as "undeserving." While the "rising tide" strategy targeting economic growth and regionally based assistance did little to raise the boats of single-mother families, subsequent policies have made the situation worse by blaming the victims of poverty. Having examined this sorry historical record, we are now ready for a closer look at the new wave of welfare "reform" for the 1990s.

Notes

1. The researchers' findings are summarized in Katherine McFate, *Poverty, Inequality, and the Crisis of Social Policy: Summary of Findings* (Washington, D.C.: Joint Center for Political and Economic Studies, 1991). Many of the original articles summarized by McFate can be found in Timothy Smeeding, Michael O'Higgins, and Lee Rainwater, eds., *Poverty, Inequality, and Income Distribution in Comparative Perspective* (London: Wheatsheaf, 1990).
2. Maria J. Hanratty and Rebecca M. Blank, "Down and Out in North America: Recent Trends in Poverty Rates in the United States and Canada," *Quarterly Journal of Economics* (February 1992).
3. Calculated by authors from U.S. Bureau of the Census, Current Population Survey, March 1994.
4. Chuck Collins, "Aid to Dependent Corporations: Exposing Federal Handouts to the Wealthy," *Dollars and Sense* (May-June 1995).
5. Robert D. Hershey, Jr., "A Hard Look at Corporate 'Welfare,' " *New York Times*, 7 March 1995, p. D1.
6. Collins, op. cit.
7. Hershey, op. cit.
8. This historical discussion is based on Nancy Rose, *Workfare or Fair Work? Women, Welfare, and Government Work Programs* (New Brunswick, NJ: Rutgers University Press, 1995), particularly chap. 1, and Nancy Rose, "Gender, Race, and the Welfare State: Government Work Programs From the 1930s to the Present," *Feminist Studies*, vol. 19, no. 7 (1993). Other useful historical sources include Mimi Abramovitz, *Regulating the Lives of Women: Social Welfare Policy from Colonial Times to the Present* (Boston: South End Press, 1988), and Linda Gordon, *Pitied But Not Entitled: Single Mothers and the History of Welfare, 1890-1935* (New York: Free Press, 1994).
9. Rose, 1995, op. cit., p. 19.
10. Teresa L. Amott and Julie A. Matthaei, *Race, Gender, and Work: A Multicultural Economic History of Women in the United States* (Boston: South End Press, revised ed., 1996).
11. Abramovitz, op. cit.
12. Jill Quadagno, *The Color of Welfare: How Racism Undermined the War on Poverty* (New York: Oxford University Press, 1994), chap. 1.
13. For a review of some of this literature, see Isabel Sawhill, "Poverty in the U.S.: Why Is It So Persistent?" *Journal of Economic Literature*, vol. 26, no. 3 (September 1988).
14. For a comprehensive view of human capital theory, see Gary Becker, *Human Capital: A Theoretical and Empirical Analysis* (New York: Columbia University Press, 1964).

15. Edward N. Wolff, *Top Heavy: A Study of the Increasing Inequality of Wealth in America* (New York: Twentieth Century Fund, 1995).
16. Chris Tilly and Randy Albelda, "It'll Take More Than a Miracle: Income in Single Mother Families in Massachusetts, 1979-87," occasional paper, University of Massachusetts-Boston, John W. McCormack Institute for Public Affairs, 1992.
17. Steve Gold, "The ABCs of Block Grants," *State Fiscal Brief,* Center for the Study of the States (Albany, NY: Nelson A. Rockefeller Institute of Government), no. 28 (March 1992).
18. Rush Limbaugh, *The Way Things Ought to Be* (New York: Pocket Books, 1993), p. 41.
19. The Heritage Foundation materials are quite misleading, if not inaccurate. See Randy Albelda, Nancy Folbre, and the Center for Popular Economics, *The War on the Poor: A Defense Manual* (New York: The New Press, 1996).
20. Christopher Georges, "Conservative Heritage Foundation Finds Recipe for Influence: Ideas and Marketing = Clout," *Wall Street Journal,* 8 August 1995, p. A10.
21. Charles A. Murray, *Losing Ground: American Social Policy, 1950-1980* (New York: Basic Books, 1994).
22. David Ellwood, *Poor Support: Poverty in the American Family* (New York: Basic Books, 1988); Peter Gottschalk and Sheldon Danziger, "Macroeconomic Conditions, Income Transfers, and Poverty," in *The Social Contract Revisited,* ed. D. Lee Bawden (Washington, D.C.: Urban Institute Press, 1984).
23. Richard Herrnstein and Charles A. Murray, *The Bell Curve: Intelligence and Class Structure in American Life* (New York: Free Press, 1994).
24. For a sampling of commentary on *The Bell Curve,* see Steven Fraser, ed., *The Bell Curve Wars* (New York: Basic Books, 1995), and Russell Jacoby and Naomi Glauberman, *The Bell Curve Debate* (New York: Times Books, 1995).
25. Claude M. Steele and Joshua Aronson, "Stereotype Threat and the Intellectual Test Performance of African Americans," *Journal of Personality and Social Psychology,* vol. 69, no. 5 (1995).
26. Margery A. Turner, Michael Fix, and Raymond J. Struyk, *Opportunities Denied, Opportunities Diminished: Racial Discrimination in Hiring,* Urban Institute report 91-9 (Washington, D.C.: Urban Institute, 1991); Marc Bendick, Jr., Charles W. Jackson, and Victor A. Reinoso, "Measuring Employment Discrimination through Controlled Experiments," *Review of Black Political Economy* (summer 1994).
27. Joleen Kirschenman and Katherine Neckerman, " 'We'd love to hire them, but . . . ': The Meaning of Race for Employers," in *The Urban Underclass,* eds. Christopher Jencks and Paul E. Peterson (Washington, D.C.: Brookings Institution, 1991). Philip Moss and Chris Tilly, " 'Soft' Skills and Race: An Investigation of Black Men's Employment Problems," *Work and Occupations,* vol. 23, no. 3 (1996).

28. Barbara F. Reskin and Heidi I. Hartmann, Women's Work, Men's Work: Sex Segregation on the Job (Washington, D.C.: National Academy Press, 1986).

29. Charles Murray, "Does Welfare Bring More Babies?" *The American Enterprise* (January/February 1994).

30. Quotes are from Hilary Stout, "GOP's Welfare Stance Owes a Lot to Prodding from Robert Rector," *Wall Street Journal*, 23 January 1995, p. A1.

31. Robert Rector, "Requiem for the War on Poverty: Rethinking Welfare After the L.A. Riots," *Policy Review Magazine* (summer 1992).

32. Heritage Foundation, *Combatting Family Disintegration, Crime, and Dependence: Welfare Reform and Beyond* (Washington, D.C.: Heritage Foundation, 1994), p. 1.

33. Albelda, Folbre, and the Center for Popular Economics, op. cit.

34. AFDC expenditures are from U.S. House Committee on Ways and Means, *Overview of Entitlement Programs, 1994 Green Book* (Washington, D.C.: Government Printing Office, 1994), p. 389; state expenditures for 1970 are from Advisory Committee on Intergovernmental Relations, *Significant Features of Fiscal Federalism, 1989 Edition*, vol. II; state expenditures for 1992 are from *Statistical Abstract of the United States, 1994* (Washington, D.C.: Government Printing Office, 1995).

35. U.S. Bureau of the Census, *Statistical Abstract of the United States* (Washington, D.C.: Government Printing Office, 1995).

36. Ibid., table 162.

37. Albelda, Folbre, and the Center for Popular Economics, op. cit. Figure for mortgage interest deduction is for 1993.

38. Calculated by authors from U.S. Bureau of the Census, Current Population Survey, March 1974 and 1994.

39. Sharon Parrott and Robert Greenstein, *Welfare, Out-of-Wedlock Childbearing, and Poverty: What is the Connection?* (Washington, D.C.: Center on Budget and Policy Priorities, 1995).

40. U.S. House Committee on Ways and Means, op. cit.

41. U.S. House Committee on Ways and Means, op. cit.

7

Lean, Mean, and Ineffective: Why 1990s-Style Welfare Reform Won't Work

AFDC, the major welfare program for low-income families in the United States from 1935 to 1996, did not work—but not for the reasons most commonly heard. Conservative authors and politicians argue that the program encouraged dependency and irresponsibility, but these criticisms are wide of the mark. In reality, AFDC did not work because it refused to address the real issues facing single-mother families: women's wages are simply not enough to support a family, and being a parent requires increased time in unpaid activities and money to meet basic needs.

Instead of facing up to this reality, welfare "reform" in the 1980s and early 1990s focused on job placement and collecting support from nonresident fathers. Frustrated by the predictable lack of success of such programs, however, state and federal governments have, in a short period of time, prescribed a host of new welfare policies.

The new state reforms are a mixed bag. In some cases, they incorporate sensible changes that work in the direction of reducing poverty, such as allowing welfare recipients to keep more of the money they earn. Yet on the whole, such positive initiatives are being overwhelmed by an avalanche of misguided, punitive policies: behavior modification as a way to reduce welfare rolls, time-limited benefits, and workfare.

The federal reform passed in 1996 is much more clearly inadequate. It emphasizes the replacement of public assistance
with earnings. In addition to changing funding from the federal
level to block grants made to states, the new law gives states full
authority with virtually no accountability. Overall, it signals a low
point in U.S. poverty policy. Neither the federal nor the state
approaches hold much promise for significantly diminishing
poverty; they amount to new ways to punish welfare recipients
and bully them off the welfare rolls. In this chapter, we focus on
the punitive aspect of the new policies. In Chapter Eight, which
lays out an alternative direction for welfare reform, we highlight
the positive steps already being taken by some states.

States' rights—or wrongs?

When AFDC was a federal program with federal rules and regulations, states were given considerable leeway in establishing eligibility requirements and benefit levels. Since the early 1990s,
states have been encouraged to expand their autonomy even further by applying for "waivers" to the federal AFDC rules. In President Clinton's first term, forty-two state legislatures passed reforms and received waivers to deviate from the federal
provisions of AFDC. For the most part, the waivers have added
sticks, not carrots, to state-level welfare policy. We discuss four
of these types of measures: the push to replace public benefits
with earnings, the extraction of child support, behavior modification, and workfare.

Working it out?

The expectation that women should work greatly shaped the
policies of the 1980s, so much so that putting women to work
has become the mainstay of welfare programs. State policies
aimed at enhancing employability spawned programs with
catchy names such as ET (Employment and Training) Choices
(Massachusetts), GAIN (Gaining Avenues to Independence, California), and REACH (Realizing Economic Achievement, New Jersey). The presumption is that women—including single mothers
—should and can do paid work, and that paid work will provide
economic independence.

Policymakers in the 1980s realized that many women on AFDC would need training or educational opportunities to get jobs. Despite limited information on the success of state programs, Congress reformed AFDC via the Family Support Act of 1988 to require states to provide education and training programs for work-eligible adult recipients whose children were three years and older (with the option of pushing this age limit down to one year and older) through the Jobs Opportunity and Basic Skills (JOBS) program.

State reform in the 1990s has taken a harder line—from enhancing employability to *requiring* work. Typically, these reforms have included both carrots and sticks, allowing recipients to keep more of their cash benefits when they do waged work, but also imposing mandatory work requirements and sanctioning recipients who do not comply.

How well has work worked out? Evaluations of the job training efforts claim mild success, but the gains have been minimal. In a recent study of four job training programs under AFDC, evaluators found that participants did increase their earnings over those of a control group that received welfare benefits without job training. Yet the earnings payoff was low indeed. Over a five-year period following the training, the gains averaged from $34 per month in San Diego's program to $20 per month in Virginia's. Further, virtually all of the gains came from shortening the length of time it took to find a job rather than from improved weekly earnings. Given the low level of earnings gains, it is not surprising that these experimental programs failed to reduce the degree to which women returned to welfare after finding employment.[1] While this study only tracks four different programs, significantly, it marks the first time welfare recipients receiving job training were tracked carefully along with a control group for a five-year period.

Why are these job programs so ineffectual? Primarily because the jobs women get typically pay too little to support themselves and their families, due to sex segregation by occupation and the time demands of childcare. Furthermore, welfare regulations are slanted against earners. Under previous federal rules, after four months of paid work, AFDC benefits were reduced almost one dollar for each dollar earned, so that gaining a job reduced one's time without boosting income by much. And although recipients get Medicaid and childcare vouchers while they are in training programs, most of the jobs they find do not provide health benefits, and government health care and childcare assistance are cut off after a year in the workforce. For many women, work does not pay. In two of the four job programs examined in the recent study, participants were *no* better off financially after five years, because earnings were exactly offset by their lost AFDC benefits.[2]

Another important reason why training programs do little to boost women's earnings is that most do not invest in the long-term—and more expensive—training required to place women in well-paying jobs. In the five-year study, only one training program, in Baltimore, resulted in higher earnings due to better-paying jobs, as opposed to earlier employment. Out of the four programs, only Baltimore's encouraged women to look and train for higher-paying jobs, even if it meant staying on AFDC longer. It was also the one program that did not yield much in the way of AFDC savings. And even the Baltimore program was not able to reduce the number of long-term recipients —women who typically have serious health, disability, or basic skill problems.[3]

Given the overwhelming evidence that low-wage work does not pay for single mothers, some states have reformed their policies to make work pay more by reducing the benefit cuts that come with earnings, and by extending childcare and Medicaid beyond the first year of employment. But unfortunately, in most states, the centerpiece of 1990s' welfare reform is *forced* and prompt employment. By early 1996, two-thirds of states had expanded JOBS participation or reduced the number of those exempt from participating, and fourteen states imposed work requirements either immediately upon receipt of AFDC or after a short period of time.[4]

While requiring paid work may move women off the welfare rolls, it does not necessarily move them out of poverty. As economist Rebecca Blank notes in an examination of low-wage entry jobs, "Essentially, unskilled women have always had access to bad jobs at bad wages, and little has changed for them over the past few decades. Their earnings opportunities are no worse, but also no better than they were one or two decades ago."[5] She concludes:

> It would be foolish for work/welfare programs to assume that women who find jobs will make steady economic progress toward substantially higher wages. Some welfare recipients will be able to follow this model (particularly those with more education), but this is unlikely to be the typical experience among women who lack high school diplomas or even among those who have a high school degree.[6]

Of course, much of the political rhetoric about work and welfare insists that single mothers have a *responsibility* to work, regardless of whether it provides a path out of poverty. But single mothers already do work! First, raising children is work. It requires time, skills, and commitment. While we as a society don't place a monetary value on it, it is work that is invaluable —and indeed, essential to the survival of our society. As one Wisconsin single mother asked sociologist Mark Rank, "I mean if you've got a family, what're you talking about lazy!? A woman is on [welfare] because she's got some children. And if she's at home and she's doing for her family, how the hell is she lazy?"[7]

Second, drawing welfare benefits *itself* requires work. Recipients must manage a generally indifferent or even hostile bureaucracy. They must master the eligibility requirements and regulations for a mix of low-income programs that, in some cases, includes Food Stamps, WIC (Women, Infants, and Children, a program of discounts on certain food necessities), Medicaid, housing subsidies, and/or SSI. The risk of getting cut off from one or another program is constant, and any change in family or employment circumstances calls for renewed wrangling with welfare's officialdom. Studies such as sociologist Ida Susser's firsthand account of life in a poor white Brooklyn neighborhood spell out the results: welfare recipiency is fraught with tension and punctuated by difficult and confusing meetings at the welfare office. Welfare officials often set up an obstacle course for recipients: long waits, demands for return visits and added documentation, and arbitrary rulings that require enormous efforts to reverse.[8]

Third, most single mothers receiving public assistance *al-*

ready do paid work. A recent study found that three-fourths of women who received any AFDC over a twenty-four-month period in the late 1980s *did* have some form of employment or were actively seeking employment.[9] In fact, combining work with welfare is and always has been a vital strategy for low-income mothers.

For the half of recipients who combine welfare and paid work, welfare substitutes for unemployment benefits, tiding over women who are between jobs (or are just starting to look for work) but have not built up enough continuous employment experience to qualify for unemployment. About 20 percent of these women earn so little that they still qualify for welfare when they work, while another 20 percent use welfare temporarily as a form of disability insurance.

Other government aid, such as unemployment benefits and workers' compensation, are rarely attacked by politicians because they are considered "well deserved." "Well deserved," in this case, means that recipients have typically worked for pay before drawing on these benefits, and most seek to work afterwards as well. But even if we accept this definition, most welfare recipients also "deserve" their benefits. Unfortunately, because of family commitments, mothers—and especially single mothers —have a much harder time accruing the continuous labor force time required to become eligible for other job-related benefits.

To the extent that this nation forces single mothers into the labor market, the costs will be borne not only by these women and their children, but also by other workers. A recent study by the Economic Policy Institute (EPI) points out that forcing welfare recipients into the labor market will have a significant side effect: driving down wages for low-skilled workers, by adding many new competitors for jobs. The EPI study makes the most *optimistic* assumption, that all welfare recipients will be able to find jobs. But employers do not hire people simply because they want work. The wage must be right, from the employer's perspective. At any given skill level, the lower the going wage, the more workers employers will want to hire. Turning that around, when workers are added to the workforce, all else being equal, employers will only be willing to hire larger numbers if the going wage is reduced. As a result, EPI researchers looked at what would have happened in 1994 if work requirements pushed

928,000 mothers off public assistance (the Urban Institute estimates that the new federal legislation will push one million families off AFDC). They concluded that this influx of new job seekers would drive the average hourly wage for the bottom third of the workforce down by 12 percent—from $5.47 to $4.82 per hour.[10]

Deadbeat dads?

In light of the limited success in reducing welfare rolls with employment, states have begun to crack down on "deadbeat dads" who owe child support, especially the fathers of children on public assistance. On the surface, requiring fathers to take responsibility for their own children seems perfectly reasonable. Certainly, society *hopes* that couples provide nurturing and loving homes, and only have children as long as they are willing to care for them. In reality, we know this is far from the truth. Many two-adult families provide woefully inadequate care—due to neglect, indifference, violence, and substance abuse, among other reasons. Further, many people—not just low-income single mothers—have a child even though they know they will have a hard time supporting him or her.

There are many families in which one parent is absent. The reasons are varied—violence, incompatibility, wanderlust. As employment has made women more independent, men have also become freer to leave.[11] As male control over family life (via the purse strings) has loosened, so has men's responsibility. Additionally, social values have made it more acceptable for women to have children out of wedlock, and divorce has become commonplace.[12]

Much like states' attempts in the 1920s and early 1930s to make adults support their aging parents, child support in the 1990s attempts to legislate family ties that have loosened at precisely the time when many men—especially young men—are seeing their earning opportunities shrink. The inflation-adjusted weekly wages of male high school graduates fell by 19 percent between 1973 and 1995.[13] And like past attempts to mandate elder support, the stepped-up child support measures will fall far short of what is needed.

According to a National Governors' Association survey, as of 1994, thirty-four states had implemented or proposed changes to increase collection of child support from noncustodial parents and/or to establish the paternity of children on welfare. Massachusetts exemplifies some of the most vigorous efforts to enforce child support payment. The state uses its new welfare reform law to sanction mothers who do not supply the absent father's full name and social security number or full name and two other specific pieces of information, even if they do not have this information. A group of women who challenged the provision in court through a class-action suit argued that they could not comply with the new reporting rules (one absent father had fled the country, while another had not been in touch for eight years), even though they supplied as much information as they had. While these women were able to obtain an injunction against the requirement, the state has not changed its law. The state has also aggressively pursued absent fathers to try to collect, even displaying the faces of "deadbeat dads" on "wanted" posters in the streets and subways. Any father who leaves his family to allow them to qualify for government assistance (including Medicaid or Food Stamps as well as cash assistance) can be punished by a fine of $200 to $600 or three months in prison.

The "collect-from-dad" approach, while politically popular, is unlikely to affect the well-being of many single-mother families. First, many absent parents who fail to pay child support are not willful scofflaws. Despite media publicity about "deadbeat dads" who refuse to take responsibility, many absent parents are unable to pay. A study done in the late 1980s found that half of Wisconsin's "deadbeat dads" had income below the poverty line for a family of one ($6,155 in 1988). An additional 20 percent had income of less than $12,310. In short, seven out of every ten noncomplying fathers were poor or nearly poor.[14] Irwin Garfinkel, professor of social work at Columbia University, comments, "If we had a perfect system and collected 100 percent of the child support, we would still only cut welfare by 25 percent."[15] You can't get blood from a stone.

Evidence suggests that strict child support enforcement will only help at the margins, and mostly for families with higher earning capacities. In 1993, 21 percent of single-mother families with incomes at or below the poverty line received child support, averaging a modest $1,551 per year. Of single-mother families who would have been in poverty without child support payments, those payments lifted only one in twenty out of poverty. Typically, those families receiving this form of interfamily income were ones in which the mothers were highly educated: half of single mothers receiving child support had at least one year of college education, whereas only one-third of those who did not receive child support had that level of education. In fact, child support helps welfare recipients least: AFDC mothers averaged a paltry $239 in child support in 1993; other single mothers received an average of $1,548.[16]

The second important limitation of child support has been the provision (prior to August 1996, a federal requirement; now, a state option) allowing a woman on welfare to keep at most $50 per month from child support, turning over the rest to the state. This provision lapses only if the support exceeds the monthly benefit, in which case a woman is no longer eligible for cash assistance. The $50 limit obviously reduces the state's welfare expenditures, but it does little to improve poor single-mother families' income. Further, it virtually eliminates any incentive for custodial parents to pressure absent parents to pay more child support, or for absent parents concerned with their family's economic well-being to increase their payments legally. Though a few states have raised the $50 limit slightly, the main "solution" to increasing compliance adopted by Massachusetts and a number of other states has been to penalize mothers who are unable to produce required identifying information about the missing father. Some states cut off all benefits to the children as well as the mother if she is unable to produce the information.

Bad attitudes: Behavior modification and punishing the recipient

A theme is beginning to emerge. Providing limited training does little to help welfare recipients earn more, so states have chosen to *require* paid employment. Measures to enforce child support have garnered little cash, so states are trying to *force* mothers to turn in absent fathers. This approach has been replicated in other areas of welfare regulation as well.

In fact, it would be fair to say that a whole new type of welfare reform has emerged in the 1990s: behavior modification. Largely driven by conservative federal social policy, states have received permission from Washington to link welfare receipt to a set of "middle-class" behaviors. Benefit receipt is contingent upon be-having. These state programs include:

- Learnfare, which suspends payment if a child misses a certain number of days of school or gets a failing grade;
- The Family Cap, which freezes benefits at their current level when another child is born to a poor mother receiving cash assistance (rather than raising benefits to reflect added costs, as was standard until recently);
- Incentives for implanting the contraceptive Norplant;
- Bridefare (or Wedfare), which gives small monetary benefits for marrying the father of a child; and
- Shotfare, in which a family loses benefits if immunization records are incomplete for any child.

While behavior modification dovetails nicely with the emphasis on individual responsibility (and blame), such programs are largely predicated on faulty assumptions about the behavior of poor families. They assume, for example, despite evidence to the contrary, that poor mothers care less about their children and whether or not they attend school than other mothers do, and that welfare mothers have more children so they can increase their benefits. Yet when Wisconsin considered extending Learn-fare provisions to cover six to twelve year olds, a report was released indicating that children in that state's AFDC families attended school, on average, only three days less per year than children in non-AFDC families (169 vs. 172).[17] Nonetheless, Wisconsin put Learnfare into effect. A 1996 study by the Wisconsin Legislative Audit Bureau concluded that Learnfare "had no detectable effect on school participation."[18]

Similarly, studies have shown no correlation between AFDC benefit levels and the rate of single parenthood, so there is no reason to believe that incremental increases in the welfare grant induce women to have additional children. Conservatives such as Charles Murray have argued that overly generous welfare benefits encourage single motherhood and therefore contribute to growing poverty (see Chapter Six). But as we saw in Table 5.1, comparisons among states suggest just the opposite relationship: the higher the benefits, the lower the poverty and the lower the birth rates.

The timing of increases in out-of-wedlock births also does not correspond to the rise and fall of AFDC benefit levels. After adjusting for inflation, benefits have fallen since the 1970s, but single motherhood has continued to grow.[19]

One factor that *does* contribute to single motherhood and welfare receipt is one that "family values" conservatives don't like to emphasize: domestic violence. A recent study of a representative sample of one state's AFDC population found that two-thirds of all adult recipients had been subject to domestic violence at the hands of a former or current husband or boyfriend —20 percent within the past twelve months.[20] These findings are consistent with other studies. A 1992 survey in the state of Washington found that 60 percent of AFDC recipients had suffered sexual or physical abuse, compared to 35 percent of a random sample of women from poor neighborhoods. Surveys of AFDC mothers in a wide range of cities and states across the country—including Hawaii; Chicago, IL; Kansas City, MO; Worcester, MA; and even Marshalltown, IA—reveal high rates of past and even present domestic violence, particularly among long-term welfare recipients.[21]

While states obsess over regulating the behavior of poor mothers, other U.S. citizens—the vast majority of whom receive some form of government aid—are not punished for the behavior of their children or for having (or not having) children, nor are they required to perform free labor, or scrutinized for their sexual behavior. Consider the tax "subsidy" currently available for middle-class and wealthy parents. In 1996, married couples with income below $86,025 received a $2,400 federal tax exemption for each child (up to two children), and most states with income taxes also allow deductions. The New Jersey Assembly, in passing its Family Cap law, declared that withholding the extra $64 a month for another child would be enough of an economic incentive not to have a child. Meanwhile, a New Jersey married couple with two children whose taxable income is $60,000 pays $1,585 a year less—or $66 per child per month—in state and federal income taxes than a married couple with the same financial situation but no children. Yet no one seriously thinks that people have more children simply to get a larger tax break. Similarly, low- to middle-income parents with wages are eligible for the Earned Income Credit—which, in 1996, was as high as

$3,600 for a family with two or more children—but no one threatens them with a withdrawal of their tax break if their children are truant. The surveillance and scrutiny to which welfare recipients are subjected would cause an outcry if directed toward any other citizen.

Workfare: Work as punishment

Workfare—requiring a welfare recipient to perform work, usually in the public or private nonprofit sector, in order to receive benefits—has been a component of many welfare reform efforts. Several states used workfare in the 1980s, and some component of workfare is now part of most new state welfare reform measures, as well as the 1996 federal law. If recipients do not find a job, they are required to perform an assigned one in order to receive benefits. If they do not perform their workfare assignment, they can be sanctioned and lose their grant. Usually states exempt some recipients from the work requirement—typically mothers of very young or disabled children.

The workfare component of welfare reform reflects the growing expectation that recipients must "work" for their money—willfully ignoring the childrearing work that they already do. After all, legislators reason, other mothers work. In addition to the *quid pro quo*, some argue that workfare gives single mothers skills they need to get paying and self-supporting jobs. Given its "make-work" nature, however, the benefits of job training via workfare are questionable. In New York City's workfare program, recipients are not assessed for their employability or skill levels. Nor are they given any training prior to being placed. As a result, of the 21,000 workfare placements as of March 1996, 29 percent were in cleaning up parks, 10 percent in cleaning up public buildings, and 7 percent in cleaning streets.[22] If these were official city jobs, they might pay well and have benefits attached, but workfare is unpaid, and workers in those placements have no rights on the job. Not surprisingly, organized labor (state workers and many contractors with the state) has typically opposed allowing the "free" labor of workfare participants in jobs under their jurisdiction. Ironically, then, the jobs in the public sector that pay decent wages and are covered by collective bargaining agreements are typically off limits under most workfare scenarios.

None of the states with workfare schemes in the 1980s found that they significantly improved the earning capacity of the women in the programs. For example, the only employment and training program West Virginia offered in the 1980s was workfare. Following nine months of receiving AFDC, workfare participants received average earnings that were a tiny $4.50 per *month* higher than AFDC recipients who had not participated in workfare.[23] The Manpower Demonstration Research Corporation (MDRC) found no statistically significant impact on employment or earnings of workfare programs for AFDC recipients in West Virginia; Cook County, IL; and San Diego, CA. MDRC researchers concluded that "there is little evidence that unpaid work experience leads to consistent employment or earning effects."[24] As part of the required evaluation for Wisconsin welfare reform waivers, John Pawasarat and Lois Quinn evaluated the Community Work Experience Program in terms of its identified goals: to reduce AFDC dependency and to increase economic self-sufficiency. They found that community work programs increased quarterly earnings for AFDC families in only two of the twenty-nine counties studied when compared to counties using a limited job search program that had little or no funding for education and training.[25]

Workfare, as implemented in many states and codified in the new federal law, precludes other forms of employment and training. For example, in Massachusetts, recipients with school-age children must perform twenty hours per week of community service after two months on cash assistance. Any education or training can only be undertaken in addition to the required twenty hours of workfare. As a result, Massachusetts community colleges are seeing their once substantial enrollments of recipients drop precipitously. At New York's City College, 5,000 students were forced to drop out because of workfare in 1996.[26] This, despite the fact that education is the surest route out of poverty for women.

Finally, workfare can be very expensive. States are currently required to provide childcare and transportation subsidies, in addition to covering the administrative costs associated with placement and monitoring. MDRC estimated the annual cost of workfare programs to be between $700 and $8,200 per filled slot in 1993. Pawasarat and Quinn found that despite Wisconsin's claim of saving over $300 million between 1988 and 1992, analysis of costs and savings using the methodology prescribed by the federal government showed substantial cost *increases* due to the workfare program. And of course, all these added costs come without any new services provided to recipients. States could—if they chose—provide effective job training rather than workfare at the same cost.

A tale of two states: The high price of success

Through federal waivers, states have been granted permission to experiment with their own welfare systems. They have implemented a variety of policy alternatives—many discussed above —aimed at promoting work, schooling, marriage, and child immunization while deterring repeated childbearing, teenage school truancy, and relocation to a state for higher benefits. Unfortunately, the reforms that states have initiated on their own have typically been more concerned with reducing the welfare rolls than with reducing poverty. And the "successes" achieved by the draconian measures are dubious in light of the quality of the lives of the low-income people subjected to them.

Wisconsin Governor Tommy Thompson and Michigan Governor John Engler were two of the strongest advocates pushing federal legislators to turn AFDC into a block grant. They pointed to the successes they achieved in their own states in reforming public assistance through "get tough" measures. But how successful have they been? A closer look at the Wisconsin and Michigan stories reveals that public assistance recipients have been the real losers.

Let's start with Michigan. In the fall of 1991, Governor Engler received legislative approval for his plan to eliminate the state's General Assistance (GA) program. GA served low-income persons not eligible for other programs, such as AFDC or SSI. At the time the program was eliminated, over 80,000 people were receiving a maximum of $160 per month from the state. The fiscal crisis of the early 1990s, coupled with the governor's political agenda, made the most vulnerable citizens of the state easy targets. Ironically, the state of Michigan ran a budget surplus in 1993 exactly equal to the cost of the GA program.

In a careful study of a sample of former GA recipients over two years, University of Michigan researchers Sandra Danziger and Sherrie Kossoudji found that the majority reported that their quality of life had become drastically worse.[27] This result is not surprising given that over half of the former recipients reported that health problems affected their ability to work. The job market in Michigan certainly did not help either. One of every three who did find a job within the first year after GA was eliminated was not employed by the end of the year. And while more than one-third of former GA recipients had at one point held a job in the high-paying manufacturing sector, of those holding jobs two years after GA was eliminated, fewer than 10 percent were in manufacturing. What's more, only 12 percent were in jobs providing health insurance. One out of every four ex-recipients was in a temporary living situation, doubling up with friends or relatives. Danziger and Kossoudji concluded that after GA ended, "The majority of people were unable to replace benefits with adequate alternative means of support. Rather than terminate programs abruptly, states should base welfare budget cuts on accurate appraisals of need and should provide transitional resources and services."[28]

Michigan's experience with GA sheds light on the possible effects of the new TANF legislation, which has also pushed many people into the labor force who are typically receiving assistance precisely because the labor market isn't working for them, through no fault of their own.

The loudest voice in the chorus for dismantling welfare is that of Governor Thompson. He takes full credit for Wisconsin's 22 percent decline in caseloads over the last decade. Just how did he do it? A recent analysis of the Wisconsin story argues that while the rolls did indeed decline, that may not all be good news. And the results in Wisconsin are not replicable in other states. Michael Wiseman, a poverty researcher at the University of Wisconsin in Madison, found that the decline in the AFDC rolls is attributable to three main factors:

- the restriction of eligibility and benefits;
- a strong state economy; and
- exceptionally large expenditures on job training programs, primarily financed by the federal government.[29]

The first of these can and is being replicated in other states. Tightened eligibility, reduced benefits, and increased rules and regulations often lead to decreased spending as people are cut from the rolls. Bureaucratic hostility and public scorn toward welfare recipients discourage current recipients from continuing their aid and deter those eligible from applying. And while the governors of states with declining rolls are tooting their horns, the drop in recipiency deserves closer scrutiny and concern. If women and their children are worse off—for example, because women are staying in abusive situations or leaving children unattended in order to go to work—then the reforms are reprehensible and costly in both human and economic terms, especially over the long haul.

The health of Wisconsin's economy and federal largesse are not reproducible. The roller coaster nature of the economy assures periodic downturns, and changes at the federal level mean large reductions in job training programs. States could, in principle, spend money on training programs to make up for the federal cuts. This is unlikely, however, since states have been reluctant even to fully match available federal funds for training and placement programs. The notion that every state can and will emulate Wisconsin is a dangerous mirage.

Further, researchers who compared the characteristics of AFDC recipients in mid-1983, prior to the reforms, to those in 1993, after many highly touted reforms, found that the profile of AFDC recipients had changed noticeably. Forty-two percent lacked a high school diploma in 1993, compared to 35 percent in 1983; a larger proportion had more than one child (57 percent in 1993 vs. 50 percent in 1983); and the percentage of recipients with a preschool child rose from 62 to 72 percent.[30] These changes suggest that "creaming" occurred initially—i.e., those who were most job-ready moved off the rolls quickly, and the harder-to-place recipients now remain.

The ultimate "unreform":
Temporary assistance to needy families

In August 1996, President Clinton signed federal legislation that abolished AFDC and, with it, the guarantee of public assistance to poor families with children. In its place is a piece of legislation that creates a block grant entitled Temporary Assistance for Needy Families (TANF). The law in question, the Personal Responsibility and Work Opportunity Reconciliation Act, bears an ironic name indeed, since it does not create any new jobs for those parents who have taken on the responsibility of raising children.

This new legislation was a Republican measure crafted as part of House Speaker Newt Gingrich's "Contract With America." In addition to a 22 percent cut in Food Stamps and Supplemental Security Income—primarily to legal immigrants—the law dramatically transforms the old AFDC legislation in four important ways:

- It ends the guarantee of cash assistance to poor families.
- It establishes a new fiscal relationship between the federal government and the states through block grants, no longer providing financial incentive for states to spend additional money on low-income families.
- It establishes a lifetime limit of sixty months (not necessarily consecutive) of assistance from federal TANF funds.
- It penalizes states that do not force a substantial portion of adults into narrowly defined work programs.

Ending welfare as we knew it

Relying on the rhetoric that states know best and that dependency is bad, federal legislators erased the right to receive public assistance. States are now free to define "neediness" and design programs however they see fit, without any accountability. They no longer have to provide cash assistance and can completely privatize their welfare systems. The lack of uniform eligibility provisions, previously provided for under the AFDC program, opens the door to the systematic disentitlement of groups that was prevalent in the years before the welfare rights movement of the 1960s and 1970s emerged. Further, states have no obligation, as they did under AFDC, to demonstrate that their programs are working—i.e., reducing or alleviating poverty among needy families with children.

Block grant = reduced funding

In 1996, the federal government spent $14 billion on the AFDC program, a total based on the amount states spent to serve eligible families. One of the major changes in the new legislation is in the area of financing—in the move from a matching grant to a block grant. Under the AFDC program, the federal government paid for at least 50 percent of AFDC benefits, while the states picked up the rest of the tab. Every time a state increased AFDC spending by one dollar, the federal government kicked in an additional dollar. The 1988 Family Support Act extended this matching grant structure to childcare costs. Childcare funding was guaranteed to every adult who participated in education and training while on welfare, as well as for a year after the recipient was no longer eligible for AFDC but was employed.

Under TANF, instead of paying for all eligible recipients, the federal government sends each state a lump sum (a block) of money to spend on welfare benefits. Childcare money has also been turned into a block grant. The amount of TANF money each state receives is based on its 1995, 1994, or 1992-1994 average federal AFDC allocation—whichever is highest. This amount will be allocated every year through 2002, and will not be adjusted for inflation or need. If the welfare rolls expand due to an economic downturn, states will not automatically receive any more money from the federal government, as they did under the AFDC program. And without entitlement status, when the funds for any given year are depleted, poor families will be left to fend for themselves.[31] While many states will receive more in TANF funds in 1997 than they did under the AFDC program in 1996 (welfare rolls were lower in 1996 than in previous years due to an improved economy and increased stigmatization of welfare receipt), the Urban Institute predicts that under block grants, states will receive $5.3 billion less over the next six years than they would have received under the old law.[32]

Under the new block grant structure, states can spend as much of their own funds as they please, but will not receive an extra penny from the federal government. In fact, TANF allows states to spend less money than they previously did on poor families. As long as a state meets federal work participation requirements (discussed below), it can cut up to one-quarter of its

1994 spending levels without any reduction in the TANF money it receives from Washington. Although states were never very generous with AFDC payments over the last two decades, the matching fund mechanism meant that states were foregoing additional federal funding every time they cut their own spending. Under TANF, no such disincentive for reduced spending exists. The Center for Budget and Policy Priorities, a Washington, D.C., think tank, estimates that states will be able to withdraw up to $40 billion from programs to poor families between 1997 and 2002, representing a 33 percent reduction of state money compared to what would have been spent under the old AFDC program.[33]

No time for mother

Assuming that women lack the motivation to get off welfare and that they become welfare dependent, the new federal legislation prohibits states from allocating TANF funds to any adult who has received such aid for sixty months over a lifetime. Yet repeated studies have shown that even without time limits, most welfare recipients *already* leave AFDC quickly, even if it is a revolving door for many. For example:

- In a study of four states that had kept good monthly case records, the Center for Law and Social Policy found that half of single-parent entrants into AFDC exited within a year of receipt, and 70 percent within two years.[34]
- Another study that tracked young women who received AFDC over ten years found that 60 percent of them left welfare within the first twelve months of AFDC receipt (88 percent had left within five years). But one-half of the women without a high school diploma who left welfare for a job returned within a year's time, and of those women with high school diplomas who were able to get off welfare because of work, half returned within two years.[35]
- Research focusing on recidivism found that 40 percent of the women who left AFDC over a twenty-four-month period in the late 1980s did so because they "earned" their way out—that is, earnings from a job made them ineligible. Yet 25 percent of those who were able to leave due to earnings returned to the rolls.[36]

For most women, public assistance is the end of the line. Not only are benefits extremely low, but the process of applying for and receiving welfare is itself often demeaning and dehumanizing. If there were viable options, many mothers would take them. Surveys and in-depth discussions with AFDC mothers suggest that it is a *last* resort, not an oasis.

Long-term, continuous welfare recipients are mostly people who face serious employment barriers, such as low education levels, little work experience, and significant health problems. Researchers investigating this issue found that single mothers were much more likely to have health problems than other mothers (12 percent vs. 4 percent). Among *long-term* recipients, 41 percent of those aged forty-five to sixty, and 20 percent of those aged thirty-five to forty-four, had disabilities or health problems that limited work.[37] Cutting off benefits for these women will not force them into the labor market. For many long-term recipients, and even for many better-off recipients, time limitations without adequate childcare, job availability, and wages are no more than a punitive measure.

States will not reach the TANF time limits until the year 2001, yet some states have instituted shorter time limits with their own funds, and many are due to reach them soon. Connecticut, the state with the shortest time limit, twenty-one months, will be the first. The thorny issues of whom to exempt and how to respond when families prove unable to find alternative income will pose important challenges.

Work, work, work

Under the new federal legislation, states must meet work participation rates in order to receive their full federal funding. The law requires all recipients to do some form of paid or unpaid work after twenty-four months of receiving benefits. States can opt to exempt recipients whose youngest child is less than one year old. Most schooling and job training do not count as "work." Further, unless states specifically opt out, adult recipients with children older than one year must perform community service (workfare) after only two months of receiving benefits. Twenty-five percent of the adults in single-parent families receiving TANF funds must work at least twenty hours per week in

1997; this participation ratio will increase to 50 percent working thirty or more hours by 2000. States can reduce their participation ratios if they reduce their caseloads.

Although previous federal provisions also had work requirements, women with disabled children or whose youngest child was less than three were exempted, and most education qualified as part of a work program. Further, under the AFDC program, anyone engaged in education and training was provided with transportation costs and childcare, neither of which are required under the new law. The Congressional Budget Office warns that the federal funding that will be required if states actually meet their work requirements—which cost money to run—is simply not there. It estimates that over the course of the new legislation's funding cycle, states will fall $12 billion short of what they would have needed under AFDC with the same participation rates, *excluding childcare costs.*

Work participation rates and a narrow definition of work, coupled with inadequate funding and "rewards" for reducing welfare rolls, create important and perverse incentives to cut people off welfare rolls (most likely through sanctions for not obeying the "rules") and to provide cheap and limited job training—the kind that has already been shown not to work. While reducing the number of recipients sounds great, it means nothing in terms of the well-being of those families no longer receiving welfare. Similarly, if the point is for women to earn their way out of poverty, reductions in education and training are counterproductive.

The bottom line

The provisions of the Personal Responsibility and Work Opportunity Reconciliation Act will increase poverty and make the lives of many low-income families qualitatively worse. On the eve of passage of the new welfare act, the Urban Institute estimated that 2.6 million people (including 1.1 million children) would be pushed into poverty by the federal legislation—including those who will lose Food Stamps and SSI income—and one million families would lose all AFDC funding.[38] It is hard to know exactly how states will handle their new authority to "manage" poverty on their own, but there are some pretty good indicators. Based on states' previous behavior, combined with the constraints the new federal legislation imposes, the results are likely to be disastrous for low-income families.

Ironically, rather than giving states a full range of choices, TANF compels them to enforce policies they never before expressed interest in implementing. It requires all states to impose time limits, although only fourteen had previously requested that provision. It has denied assistance to legal immigrants, even though no state proposed that restriction under the waiver system.[39]

In addition to the mandated restrictions, there are other good reasons to think that state policies will get harsher under block grants than under the old waiver system. Because federal matching money for the kinds of activities (such as job training and childcare) that allow women to go to work will no longer be available, and because the very programs that provide vital support to women entering low-wage jobs (like extending medical benefits or childcare to recently employed recipients) are especially costly, states are unlikely to finance programs to help keep women at work when they have to pay the entire bill.

What's more, the financial pressure on states is sure to get worse. Even a small economic downturn and resulting unemployment will increase poverty, and there are no assurances now that this increase will be met with more money from the federal government. Recessions place enormous pressure on states to cut, not increase, spending on poor families and children, since tax revenues fall, due to decreased income and sales tax, just as needs increase. Moreover, because states are legally required to balance their budgets, their needs cannot be met through deficit spending. Spending on poor families, including childcare and medical benefits, are very likely candidates for state cuts.

Unchecked state authority to limit who receives assistance and the imposition of time limits could lead to a "race to the bottom" among the states. For example, if one state imposes harsh new restrictions, policymakers in other states may follow suit to avoid the possibility of attracting migrants in search of public assistance. Lacking federal oversight, extreme welfare reform in one state could spread throughout the country.[40]

One size does not fit all

While we have taken many of the new welfare measures to task, we acknowledge that some very serious issues concerning single motherhood face the states and the country as a whole. Yet many of these problems—such as fourteen- and fifteen-year-olds having children, or homemakers with little formal education finding themselves job hunting in a depressed labor market—cannot and should not be addressed with sweeping policies that apply much more of the stick than the carrot. For these cases, much of the welfare reform currently being implemented will probably not be effective. Teenage pregnancy is not the result of welfare programs, and welfare reform's proposed "incentives" fail to address the complex issues young women face today. Similarly, without substantial training or education, some women will not be able to find jobs at all, let alone jobs that pay a living wage. And it is extremely difficult to undertake a serious discussion of the problems of long-term welfare recipients while policymakers continue to paint all welfare mothers with the same brush, deny the dramatic changes in family structure, ignore or devalue the work involved in childrearing, and leave unchallenged women's unequal earning capacity in the paid labor market.

Each woman comes to the welfare system for her own particular reasons—a divorce, a layoff, an increase in rent, or a child who has been sick for a long time. Likewise, women find a variety of ways to leave—a marriage, a family member who can do childcare regularly, a borrowed car that is reliable, or a decent paying job. Because of this, welfare reform needs to be flexible to accommodate a variety of circumstances. Still, there are some basic commonalities that can help shed light on the direction welfare reform should take to reduce poverty among women and their children. Every mother wants the best for her children. In this way, mothers who receive public assistance are no different from other mothers. Women who apply for benefits do so precisely because they cannot raise their children on the income they receive from a job or from other family members.

There are also vital safety issues to consider. The high incidence of domestic violence among women who turn to public assistance puts into question both the presumed reasons why women seek assistance and the efficacy of recent changes. While policymakers would like to assume that time-limited benefits will compel women to replace assistance with earnings, they may have an effect no one would like to see. Men who physically and sexually abuse women or their children who currently receive public assistance often feel threatened by the economic control their partners would gain if they received income on their own through earnings. Such men often refuse to allow women and girls to work, or even to participate successfully in training programs or employment.[41] Further, women who have experienced abuse are more likely to have used welfare discontinuously than other women. Women who need public assistance in order to escape violent situations may well need more than sixty months over their lifetime to get on their feet and find safe housing. If abusive partners stalk women and their children, as is often the case, time limits may actually serve to place undue pressure on AFDC recipients, forcing them into potentially dangerous situations.

What might real welfare reform look like? That is the topic of the next chapter.

Notes

1. Daniel Friedlander and Gary Burtless, *Five Years After: The Long-term Effects of Welfare-to-Work Programs* (New York: Russell Sage Foundation, 1995).
2. Ibid.
3. Ibid.
4. Center for Law and Social Policy, "Updated Waiver Information (Working Draft)" (Washington, D.C.: Center for Law and Social Policy, 1995).
5. Rebecca M. Blank, "Outlook for the U.S. Labor Market and Prospects for Low-Wage Entry Jobs," in *The Work Alternative: Welfare Reform and the Realities of the Job Market*, eds. Demetra Smith Nightingale and Robert H. Haveman (Washington, D.C.: The Urban Institute, 1995), pp. 62-63.
6. Ibid., p. 63.
7. Mark R. Rank, *Living on the Edge: The Realities of Welfare in America* (New York: Columbia University Press, 1994), p. 122.
8. Ida Susser, *Norman Street: Poverty and Politics in an Urban Neighborhood* (New York: Oxford University Press, 1982).
9. Roberta Spalter-Roth, Beverly Burr, Heidi Hartmann, and Lois Shaw, *Welfare That Works: The Working Lives of AFDC Recipients* (Washington, D.C.: Institute for Women's Policy Research, 1995). This result has been confirmed by several researchers. For example, one study

using a different data set found that over 50 percent of AFDC recipients held a job over a thirty-six-month period in the mid-1980s (Kathleen Mullan Harris, "Work and Welfare Among Single Mothers in Poverty," *American Journal of Sociology*, vol. 99, no. 2 [September 1993]).

10. Lawrence Mishel and John Schmitt, "Cutting Wages by Cutting Welfare: The Impact of Reform on the Low-Wage Labor Market," briefing paper, Economic Policy Institute, Washington, D.C., October 1995.
11. See Barbara Ehrenreich, *The Hearts of Men: American Dreams and the Flight from Commitment* (Garden City, NJ: Anchor Press, 1984).
12. Teresa Castro Martin and Larry L. Bumpass, "Recent Trends in Marital Disruption," *Demography*, vol. 26, no. 1 (1989).
13. Lawrence Mishel, Jared Bernstein, and John Schmitt, *The State of Working America, 1996-97* (Armonk, NY: M.E. Sharpe, 1997).
14. Daniel Meyer and Steven Garasky, "Custodial Fathers: Myths, Realities, and Child Support Policies," *Journal of Marriage and the Family*, vol. 55 (February 1993).
15. Rick Bragg, "Georgia, Passing Child Support, Discovers Its Potential and Limits," *New York Times*, 14 April 1995, p. A1.
16. These averages include those not receiving any child support at all.
17. Lucy Williams, "The Ideology of Division: Behavior Modification Welfare Reform Proposals," *Yale Law Journal*, vol. 102, no. 3 (1992).
18. Dirk Johnson, "Wisconsin Welfare Effort on Schools is a Failure, Study Says," *New York Times*, 19 May 1996.
19. Lawrence Mishel and Jared Bernstein, *The State of Working America: 1994-95* (Armonk, NY: M.E. Sharpe, 1994).
20. Mary Ann Allard, Randy Albelda, Mary Ellen Colten, and Carol Cosenza, *In Harm's Way? Domestic Violence, AFDC Receipt, and Welfare Reform in Massachusetts* (Boston: University of Massachusetts-Boston, 1997).
21. Jody Raphael, *Domestic Violence: Telling the Untold Welfare-to-Work Story* (Chicago: Taylor Institute, 1995), and Ellen Bassuk, Angela Browne, and John Buckner, "Single Mothers and Welfare," *Scientific American* (October 1995).
22. Liz Krueger and John Seley, "The Return of Slavery: Lessons from Workfare in New York City," *Dollars and Sense* (November/December 1996).
23. David Greenberg and Michael Wiseman, "What Did the Work-Welfare Demonstrations Do?" discussion paper DP 969-92, University of Wisconsin-Madison, Institute for Research on Poverty, 1992.
24. Thomas Brock, David Butler, and David Long, "Unpaid Work Experience for Welfare Recipients: Findings and Lessons from MDRC Research," Manpower Demonstration Research Corporation, New York, 1993.
25. John Pawasarat and Lois Quinn, *Wisconsin Welfare Employment Experiments: An Evaluation of the WEJT and CWEP Programs* (Milwaukee: University of Wisconsin-Milwaukee, Employment and Training Institute, 1993).

26. Krueger and Seley, op. cit.
27. Sandra Danziger and Sherrie Kossoudji, *What Happened to Former GA Recipients? The Second Interim Report of the General Assistance Termination Project* (Ann Arbor: University of Michigan, School of Social Work, 1994).
28. Ibid., p. 13.
29. Michael Wiseman, "State Strategies for Welfare Reform: The Wisconsin Story," discussion paper DP 1066-95, University of Wisconsin-Madison, Institute for Research on Poverty, 1995.
30. Maria Cancian and Daniel Meyer, "A Profile of Wisconsin Welfare Recipients: Baseline Data," *Focus*, vol. 18, no 1 (1996): 58.
31. There is a contingency fund that can be tapped by states during a recession, although the fund is small (it contains $5 billion over five years) compared to the increased spending of $6 billion on AFDC during the 1990-1992 recession (David Super, Sharon Parrott, Susan Steinmetz, and Cindy Mann, *The New Welfare Law* [Washington, D.C.: Center for Budget and Policy Priorities, 1996]).
32. Urban Institute, *Potential Effects of Congressional Welfare Reform Legislation*, Washington, D.C., 1996.
33. Super, *et al.*, op. cit.
34. Mark Greenberg, *Beyond Stereotypes: What State AFDC Studies on Length of Stay Tell Us About Welfare as a "Way of Life"* (Washington, D.C.: Center for Law and Social Policy, 1993).
35. Ibid.
36. Rebecca Blank and Patricia Ruggles, "Short-Term Recidivism Among Public-Assistance Recipients," *American Economic Review*, vol. 84, no. 2 (1994).
37. Barbara Wolfe and Steven Hill, "The Health, Earnings Capacity, and Poverty of Single-Mother Families," in *Poverty and Prosperity in the USA in the Later Twentieth Century*, eds. Dimitri B. Papadimitriou and Edward N. Wolff (New York: Macmillan Press, 1993).
38. Urban Institute, op. cit.
39. This includes waivers from January 1992 through February 1996. Center for Law and Social Policy, "Updated Waiver Information," Washington, D.C., March 1996.
40. Steve Savner and Mark Greenberg, *The CLASP Guide To Welfare Waivers: 1992-1995* (Washington, D.C.: Center for Law and Social Policy, 1995), p. 6.
41. Jody Raphael, "Domestic Violence and Welfare Receipt: Toward a New Feminist Theory of Welfare Dependency," *Harvard Women's Law Journal*, vol. 19 (spring 1996).

8

Creating Real Welfare Reform

Ending poverty and achieving women's economic equality are clear goals, but getting there will take time. Meanwhile, the lives of many women and children hang in the balance. Welfare reform debates have so far been couched in limited terms, posing the choice between attacking public benefits or defending the existing system. While it is important to preserve the safety net, it is equally important to make sure that welfare reform gives people a chance to get out of poverty for good.

First and foremost, welfare reform should "do no harm." Its primary purpose should be to end poverty, not to punish the poor. Further reforms to the current welfare system would make life more bearable for those who currently do receive assistance, as well as increase recipients' chances of improving their economic status and staying off welfare. In this chapter, we start by proposing such reforms to the welfare system. In Chapter Nine, we go on to suggest a much broader set of reforms that address the true welfare of families in the United States.

The changes we propose in these two chapters will not end poverty, wipe out gender inequality, or solve the tension between work and family; in that sense, they are modest. But in the current, constrained political context, they are quite ambitious. They extend far beyond the parameters of most political discussions today, and to some they may seem like "pie in the sky." We know that. But we also see these proposals as a vision for the 21st century. To help guide us toward that vision, in Chapter Ten we present a road map—four political strategies for achieving the platforms introduced in Chapters Eight and Nine.

The outlines of real federal welfare reform

Even though Congress has dismantled federal responsibilities toward poor mothers, we argue that our country should be moving in precisely the opposite direction. The eligibility rules and benefit levels of Social Security, Food Stamps, SSI, and veteran's benefits are all set at the federal level; there is no reason for public assistance to needy families to be any different. This is not to say that states should have no flexibility in the provision of benefits or that they should not reflect differences in the cost of living. Both these measures are easy to accomplish within a program of real welfare reform.[1]

The eight proposals below are neither new nor unusual. Several of the provisions have been proposed by some states, and a few are already in operation. What distinguishes our list of reforms from those discussed in the previous chapters is that we place the emphasis on establishing positive incentives, broadening the scope of welfare, and standardizing a basic set of benefits and rules in the program across the states.

1. Standardize and expand program eligibility

States are now free to define eligibility as they please. The limited resources provided by the federal government and the fiscal constraints faced by states make it unlikely that many states will *increase* the number of poor families that are eligible for assistance. Wider eligibility is only fair, however. Under the old AFDC system, poor children in families with two able-bodied adults were not eligible if their parents worked more than 100 hours a month or did not have a prior work history. Yet in an economy where many of the fastest-growing jobs are those that pay wages close to the minimum, more and more two-adult working families are poor. In 1994, for example, 7 percent of married-couple families *with at least one worker* and a child under the age of six were poor.[2] Among wage-earning, single-mother families, even those with a year-round, full-time worker, a significantly larger percentage are poor, ranging from 11 percent among such families with at least one child under age eighteen, to 17 percent for families with at least one child under six.[3] *All* needy families with children should be eligible for cash assistance or in-kind benefits on the same basis, regardless of whether one or both parents are in the home, and regardless of which state they reside in.

2. Establish a minimum benefit, then index it to inflation

Even before states were given free rein to fashion their own welfare systems, AFDC benefits were embarrassingly low. Cash benefits, even coupled with Food Stamps, are woefully inadequate to support a family. Table 8.1 lists the maximum level of cash benefits for a family of three in all fifty states and Washington, D.C., in January 1996 and October 1987 (adjusted for inflation) under the AFDC program. There are two important things to notice. First, the benefit levels vary tremendously among the states and, for the most part, are extremely low. The payments range from $120 (or $1,440 a year) in Mississippi to $923 (or $11,076 a year) in Alaska. In the median benefit state (the state exactly in the middle of the highest and lowest paying states)—New Mexico—the maximum monthly benefit for a family of three is $389, or $4,668 per year, which is 40 percent of the poverty line. While there are certainly very different costs of living across the fifty states, they do not vary as much as benefits do. The second bit of important information conveyed in Table 8.1 is the degree to which states have allowed benefit levels to fall over the last ten years. In all but five states, AFDC benefits dropped between 1987 and 1996. The median state saw a decline of 25.2 percent, and two-thirds of all the states let AFDC benefits slide 20 percent or more. By way of comparison, average hourly earnings have fallen by 4 percent over the same period.

In the United States, a national minimum wage sets a floor for what workers may earn; why not set a comparable social wage floor for what a family may receive when its adult members cannot work? Boosting benefits and establishing a benefit floor would go a long way toward improving the lives of poor women and children, but in order to maintain its value, that floor must

136 Glass Ceilings and Bottomless Pits

Table 8.1   The Fragmented Welfare States of America

Maximum AFDC benefit level for a family of three and percentage change for fifty states and Washington, D.C., 1987 and 1996 (adjusted for inflation)

	October 1987	January 1996	Percent change in benefits, 1987–1996
Alabama	$ 163	$164	0.6%
Alaska	1,034	923	−12.1
Arizona	405	347	−16.6
Arkansas	279	204	−36.8
California	874	607	−44.0
Colorado	478	421	−13.5
Connecticut	710	636	−11.6
D.C.	523	420	−24.6
Delaware	441	338	−30.4
Florida	365	303	−20.3
Georgia	363	280	−29.7
Hawaii	678	712	4.8
Idaho	420	317	−32.5
Illinois	472	377	−25.3
Indiana	398	288	−38.1
Iowa	526	426	−23.5
Kansas	529	429	−23.3
Kentucky	272	262	−3.9
Louisiana	262	190	−38.1
Maine	559	418	−33.8
Maryland	496	373	−32.9
Massachusetts	704	565	−24.7
Michigan	622	459	−35.4
Minnesota	735	532	−38.1
Mississippi	166	120	−38.1
Missouri	389	292	−33.4
Montana	496	425	−16.7
Nebraska	483	364	−32.8
Nevada	449	348	−29.0
New Hampshire	671	550	−22.0
New Jersey	586	424	−38.1
New Mexico	365	389	6.3
New York	686	577	−19.0
North Carolina	358	272	−31.5
North Dakota	512	431	−18.9
Ohio	427	341	−25.2
Oklahoma	403	307	−31.4
Oregon	428	460	6.9

continued

Table 8.1   The Fragmented Welfare States of America (continued)

	October 1987	January 1996	Percent change in benefits, 1987–1996
Pennsylvania	$504	$421	19.7%
Rhode Island	662	554	−19.4
South Carolina	276	200	−38.1
South Dakota	506	430	−17.6
Tennessee	220	185	−18.7
Texas	254	188	−35.2
Utah	519	426	−21.9
Vermont	833	650	−28.1
Virginia	402	354	−13.5
Washington	680	546	−24.5
West Virginia	344	253	−35.9
Wisconsin	714	517	−38.1
Wyoming	497	360	−38.1
Median state	$493	$389	−25.2%

Note: Benefits are adjusted using the CPI-U to 1996 dollars.

Sources: For 1987, U.S. Department of Health and Human Services, *Characteristics of State Plans for Aid to Families With Dependent Children, 1988 Edition* (1988), p. 373. For January 1996, Congressional Research Service on the basis of a telephone survey of the states.

be indexed to inflation. The main reason poverty rates for people sixty-five years and older are much lower than children's poverty rates is that Social Security and SSI benefits have not eroded with inflation.

3. Make work pay

Under the previous AFDC program, when a woman receiving welfare took a job, she lost her benefits almost dollar for dollar after four months of employment.[4] She retained her health care benefits and received a childcare subsidy, but only for one year after her earnings made her ineligible for cash benefits. Under those rules, for most women with children, going to work just didn't pay. The loss of health benefits and childcare subsidies is often cited as a reason why so many women return to welfare. A

$6-an-hour job at thirty hours a week is more than enough to push a woman off welfare—but not out of poverty. Yet a woman with small children probably can't work more than thirty hours a week. At $6 an hour—85¢ above the 1997 minimum wage— her yearly earnings are $9,360 *before* she pays for the new costs of going to work—Social Security tax, clothing, and transportation. The Earned Income Credit and Food Stamps help boost total family income considerably, but even so, a family of three will end up with income near the poverty line. After a year, if a woman loses her health benefits and her childcare subsidy runs out, even the meager level of welfare benefits can begin to look good. At a minimum, she doesn't have to find daycare for her children, and if one of them gets sick, he or she is entitled to health care.

One way to make work pay is to reduce the earnings penalty for welfare recipients who find a job. That way, when welfare recipients do work, they get to keep their earnings as well as some portion of their benefits—until the family is well out of poverty.

As of February 1996, thirty-four states had reformed their welfare systems to make work pay. States accomplish this differently, but in all cases, women with earnings get to keep more of this income as they go to work. And if implemented well, this seems to help. An experiment in Illinois allows recipients to keep two-thirds of their gross wages before counting earnings against the welfare grant. Employment rates in the program are currently 18.6 percent of the caseload, compared to a previous high of 6 percent.[5] Unfortunately, the sixty-month limit imposed by TANF might jeopardize this important work incentive, since making work pay prolongs the period during which families collect cash assistance.

4. Expand health and child services

The biggest challenge faced by most women receiving welfare is *not* getting off "the dole"—it's *staying* off. Recidivism rates are high, especially among women who leave welfare due to increased earnings. One important way to make work continue to pay—and not just for welfare mothers—is to assure *all* families health care and childcare subsidies. One full year of Medicaid for children and childcare subsidies after leaving AFDC proved an inadequate transition period for many to become financially secure. The Clinton administration pursued a universal health plan in 1993 and 1994, but since then, discussions of affordable, universal health care have all but disappeared from the national debate. This country has not even begun a national dialogue on childcare. For mothers, however, both supports are vital if they are expected to do paid work.

Forty percent of the states have reformed their welfare systems to either expand or extend medical assistance or childcare beyond the federal provisions. Yet states must be prepared to fund these programs. The new block grant system threatens the positive steps already made in this direction. As states have less money to provide the same amount of services, they will seek ways to cut back. Medical and child services are easy targets.

5. Improve the child support system

Legislation to track down "deadbeat dads" sails easily through legislatures and has been signed into law in state after state. Under the old federal law—a provision many states have opted to keep—welfare recipients were allowed to keep only the first $50 each month (or $600 a year) of any child support payments. The rest went to the state and federal governments as reimbursement for AFDC payments to the family. If the father didn't pay on time, the family didn't even get $50. States typically cracked down on parents who did not pay the full amount of court-ordered child support to make sure that they paid more than $50 per month. But while the state defrayed some of its costs, families depending on welfare were not much better off. The new federal law doesn't even require that $50 go to the family, and few states have raised their limits on how much recipients can keep.

To make child support work for welfare recipients, at a minimum, recipients should be able to keep the entire amount, without any reduction in benefits, until the family has a decent income. In addition, welfare mothers should be able to keep child support even if it is paid late. The state shouldn't benefit, and children shouldn't lose out, just because Dad didn't pay on time.

The idea of child support insurance also has merit. Under such a plan, the state would pay the family a guaranteed amount for child support. If the father paid more than the guaranteed amount, the family would get what he paid. But if he paid less, the state would make up the difference. This makes sense because fathers absent from families receiving welfare are usually poor themselves, so the amount that can be gleaned directly from child support is quite limited. New York and Wisconsin established child support insurance systems in the mid-1980s, but Wisconsin Governor Thompson dropped the program when he came into office, and New York never fully funded its program.[6]

Welfare recipients might be better off under a child support insurance system, but that depends on how it is designed. In some proposals, the assured benefit would count dollar for dollar against the welfare grant, leaving recipients *worse off* than they are now, since they would also lose eligibility for Medicaid and childcare at lower earning levels than they do now. And in other proposals, mothers wouldn't qualify for benefits unless a child support order was in place. Though 75 percent of divorced or remarried mothers had such orders in 1990, only half of all separated mothers and only one-quarter of never-married mothers had child support orders.[7] The state has the jurisdiction over the establishment and enforcement of orders, but often doesn't get around to it for welfare recipients.

On the other hand, an insurance plan could be a plus if it increased income, protected Medicaid and childcare eligibility, and guaranteed support even if the state hadn't established a child support order. Of course, child support insurance doesn't help children who live in two-parent families or whose fathers are dead. Nevertheless, well-designed child support insurance would be a first step toward a much needed child *allowance*—a guaranteed income for all children.

6. Support education and training for jobs that pay a living wage

The Job Opportunities and Basic Skills (JOBS) program, initiated by the 1988 Family Support Act, provided matching federal funds to states and required them to offer a range of basic education and skills training programs to welfare recipients. It also mandated that increasing percentages of recipients had to participate in training or work on a regular basis, meaning at least twenty hours per week. But the program failed to live up to the expectations inspired by its passage. In 1996, JOBS was abolished and, along with several job training programs, folded into a block grant.

As reported in Chapter Seven, research on AFDC demonstration projects implemented throughout the 1980s showed that education and training only marginally improved employment and earnings. Nothing in that research should have led anyone to believe that the Family Support Act would have a major impact, and certainly not in the first several years. The economic tailspin of the late 1980s and early 1990s further limited the results of JOBS. Experience to date teaches us these lessons:

- Education and training won't lead to jobs if the jobs are not there. The states with the most success in their welfare-to-work programs are ones experiencing robust economic growth.[8]
- States have never been willing to spend as much money as is necessary to bring in the full amount of federal education and training funding available. In 1994–1995, for example, states forfeited just under $250 million in federal funds—23 percent of the total allocated—because they were unwilling to come up with the matching funds needed to qualify for the full federal allocation.[9] Ironically, three of the four biggest forfeiters were states with Republican governors making political hay by getting tough on welfare: California let $41 million go, Illinois decided to forego $21 million, and Michigan gave up $17 million.
- Without a significant investment in the training and supports single mothers need (for example, childcare and transportation), work programs affect earnings very little. In other words, unless states are willing to make an investment in significant training (such as postsecondary education or working directly with employers to provide skills needed in local labor markets), forcing mothers to work is a waste of money. States might save money—and recipients would benefit comparably —if there were no mandatory job training component.

One of the few bright spots in the states' education and training records for AFDC mothers has been access to postsecondary education, one of the best ways for single mothers to escape poverty. Unfortunately, states are now restricting this area directly and indirectly, and the opportunity for higher education may be completely lost with the enforcement of time-limit or workfare requirements, since they do not exempt women in education and training programs.

Education and training programs are crucial to addressing the long-term ability of poor mothers to support themselves and their children. At a minimum, however, the programs can only work if women have choices that recognize their existing skills and abilities, if vital services like childcare are provided, and if the jobs women are training for actually exist. Quality education and training are effective in helping women leave poverty, but they require a serious financial commitment because the programs that work best typically cost more and require more time to complete.

7. Provide comprehensive assessment and services for parents and children who receive welfare, tailoring assistance to individual needs

Most women resort to welfare not because they don't want to hold a job, but because they can't. While many simply lack childcare, transportation, or training, others have much larger problems associated with collapses in their family networks and support systems, or depletion of their family's internal resources. Abusive home situations, depression and other mental health disorders, homelessness, chemical abuse, physical disabilities, and lack of coping skills are not uncommon among women seeking cash assistance. Poverty takes its toll on self-esteem and health. Further, being poor often makes even small problems harder to solve because of a lack of financial resources. The "quick fix" reforms recently adopted by Congress and many state legislatures do not address these issues, and in some cases, make them worse. The solutions become even more elusive when women are reluctant to reveal their problems for fear of losing their children to the foster care system. Time limits, workfare, mandatory training, and requirements to disclose paternity information might cause further harm to children and their mothers. Rather than this punitive barrage, support services— linking recipients to psychological services, drug treatment programs, or housing assistance—are a vital first step toward economic security.

Welfare offices are notoriously "user unfriendly." Changing the climate at welfare offices is necessary to make any welfare reform work. Caseworkers could use the application process as an interactive exploration of the barriers to finding stable employment that applicants face. Intensive case management may not be financially feasible for most states, but certainly states could identify target populations and begin there.

Utah recently enacted reforms in which a key component allowed case managers to work with every client to provide the individual set of services they needed. In doing so, they discovered their current staff was not prepared to handle some cases that required additional training and specialization. Welfare offices also became aware of the lack of mental health facilities and shelters for low-income women. Utah has only implemented changes based on these findings in three state offices, so it is too early to evaluate the results—but the initiative seems promising.[10]

8. Improve state flexibility and monitoring

While the federal government needs to set a higher baseline standard of welfare support, states can and should be able to build on this standard, with sufficient flexibility to try different approaches for providing services and reforms. The old waiver process, which required evaluation of any state deviation from federal rules, should be reinstituted. It would assure that states provide a minimum level of benefits and services, and at the same time, would serve as an important way for states to share the "best practices." A welfare system combining solid minimum guarantees, space for experimentation and improvement that recognizes the diverse needs of the welfare population, and a fundamental respect for the work entailed in caring for children offers the best prospects for really reducing poverty.

Yeah, but . . . ?

The eight proposals discussed here can be criticized for asking both too much and too little. We address the latter criticism by presenting a much broader set of reforms in the next chapter. Before moving on, however, it is worth discussing why the reforms presented here are a reasonable short-term strategy.

True, the overall tendency in welfare reform has been toward less public commitment and more stringent rules. But one reason why our eight reforms are viable is because most of them are already being tried. States are experimenting and building up a track record for these models.

Second, these reforms address the real reasons why welfare has been ineffective in the past, and therefore provide real solutions. Punitive welfare reform in the 1990s was driven mainly by a short-term political gain. It was based on and promulgated a set of myths about poor people that played on deep racial, gender, and income divisions. The drive to reform welfare, however, also tapped the genuine economic anxiety felt by many families. The time squeeze on all families, the decline in men's wages, and increases in income and wealth inequality have helped conservative politicians win support for dismantling the meager welfare system that was in place in the early 1990s. The call to push welfare mothers into the labor market resonated in light of the rapid flux of all mothers into the labor force. Attacking the provisions of assistance—small as they were—to very poor families, all the while enlisting the rage of poor and near-poor families who did not get comparable assistance yet were struggling to make ends meet, was a political coup.

But in practice, punitive welfare reform will flood the low end of the labor market with additional hungry competitors, further undermining low-income families' economic security. Such reforms will only exacerbate, not reduce, the economic problems these families experience. In short, while the political context for real welfare reform may not exist right now, the economic context does.

The current thrust of welfare reform is toward paid employment. Single mothers are being told that they need to rely on themselves or working spouses, rather than on the government. The message is, "Get married, stay married, and work!" Yet the source of many American families' economic anxiety—which is easily used as a wedge to push for punitive reforms—is precisely the inability of paid employment to support families and, at the same time, allow people to take care of family members. Ironically, the solutions proposed for poor mothers aren't working for two-parent families, either. While we think this constitutes a recipe for policy failure, it is also an opportunity to open a much broader national discussion about the nature of work and the role of families.

The eight points presented here will reconstruct a set of programs to alleviate and reduce poverty. Providing a uniform income floor, below which no family can fall, is a necessity in a society where unemployment exists and the level of domestic violence is far too high. When the job market and families fail to provide for basic needs, women and children require support until they are able to be economically independent. The majority of welfare recipients who want paid work need preparation and supports that will help them make work pay. Reknitting the safety net in this way will empower low-income women and families. It will give them some control over their economic situation, which in turn will help create the space for further political action. These are minimal goals, but very important ones.

To address change beyond this basic level, we offer a more sweeping set of reforms in the following chapter.

Notes

1. For example, if poverty threshold incomes were set to reflect housing costs and childcare expenses, eligibility and benefit levels could be pegged to poverty thresholds.
2. U.S. Bureau of the Census, *Income, Poverty and Valuation of Noncash Benefits: 1994* (Washington, D.C.: Government Printing Office, 1996), table C-2.
3. Ibid., P60-89, table 10.
4. AFDC recipients got to keep $120 plus one-third of their additional earnings each month for the first four months they had earnings. For the next eight months, they got to keep $120 of their earnings in addition to their AFDC benefits, but benefits were then reduced dollar for dollar. After one year, recipients got to keep $90 of their earnings before benefits were reduced. In short, AFDC mothers faced a "marginal tax rate" (i.e., the amount of assistance they lost for each additional dollar earned) of 100 percent after four months.
5. Phone conversation with Joseph Antolin, deputy director of the Illinois Department of Public Aid, June 4, 1996.
6. Irwin Garfinkel, Marygold S. Melli, and John G. Robertson, "Child Support Orders: A Perspective on Reform," *The Future of Children,* vol. 4, no. 1 (spring 1994): 84-100.
7. Daniel Meyer, "Alternatives to Welfare Income: The Current Child Support System," *Focus* (Madison, WI: Institute for Research on Poverty), vol. 17, no. 1 (summer 1995): 51-52.

8. See, for example, Michael Wiseman, "State Strategies for Welfare Reform: The Wisconsin Story," discussion paper DP 1066-95, University of Wisconsin-Madison, Institute for Research on Poverty, 1995, and LaDonna Pavetti and Amy-Ellen Duke, "State Welfare Reform Efforts" (Washington, D.C.: Urban Institute, 1996).

9. U.S. Department of Health and Human Services, *Title IV-F Jobs Allocations and Amounts Received by States, Fiscal Years 1992, 1993, & 1994* (1995), table 3.

10. Center for Law and Social Policy, "Welfare Reform Without a Lifetime Limit: The Experiences of Utah, Minnesota and Iowa," *Family Matters* (Washington, D.C.), vol. 7, no. 4 (fall 1995) and vol. 8, no. 1 (winter 1996).

9

It's Not Just Welfare: Policies as if Families Really Mattered

Welfare reform directed only at those who receive benefits is only a first step. Federal and state policymakers can't really tackle the mounting financial problems associated with the Medicaid program until they confront the entire health care system and reform health care for everyone. So, too, with cash assistance, childcare, and job training. Real welfare reform must recognize that families and family structures have changed, but that the U.S. job structure still has an implicit bias toward families with a full-time caregiver at home. Real welfare reform requires comprehensive family policies to level the playing field for families with young children, regardless of the number of adults in those families or their wages.

What is needed—not just for poor single mothers, but for all families—are reforms in childcare, wages, and jobs. Welfare as we knew it—income transfers to families in need—will still be necessary, but the need will be dramatically reduced if the government and employers begin to resolve the contradictions many women currently face.

Lest the checklist of policies that follows be dismissed as a frivolous fantasy, we hasten to point out that the hard-nosed governments of Western Europe have adopted similar policy packages. "Family policy" is an unfamiliar term in the United States because our family-friendly public policies are so few and far between, but it forms an integral and accepted part of European society. Most Western European nations offer universally available childcare, extensive paid parental leaves, child and housing allowances to supplement the income of families with children, universal health coverage, and government-guaranteed child support for single parents. To see where we as a nation might go, it is useful to start with a brief examination of the policies of these other countries.

Tell me I'm not dreaming: Family policy in Western Europe

In the decades since World War II, the countries of Western Europe, explicitly recognizing that raising children takes time and money, have created government policies to support families. Different countries have pursued different approaches. The Scandinavian countries and France have promoted women's paid work, providing services such as childcare to encourage paid labor, while tying many social welfare benefits to current or recent employment. Germany and some other countries in continental Europe have instead stayed closer to the "male bread-winner" model, but offer generous benefits to families who lack an employed breadwinner. Despite these variations, most of the countries of Western Europe offer a package that includes the following:[1]

- *Child or family allowances.* These are cash payments to families with children, typically available to all families at a fixed amount per child. Some countries (for example, France and Denmark) offer higher allowances to poorer families, and the amounts can be substantial: in France, a family with two small children and wages of $13,000 would receive $6,000 a year in allowances.[2]
- *Government-guaranteed child support.* Many Western European countries provide government guarantees of child support to deal with situations where absent parents fail—or are unable—to pay. In most cases, the government guarantee is small (about $1,500 per year), designed to supplement paid work rather than to replace it.[3]

- *Paid parental leave.* European countries have adopted two complementary types of parental leave policies. First, upon childbirth, mothers have the right to leave work for three months (in Luxembourg) to three years (in France and Germany) without losing job rights or seniority. Second, governments and employers together generally pay the mother full or nearly full wages for part of this period (typically, at least three to six months). Most countries offer some parental leave to fathers as well, and Norway and Sweden offer longer total leave times if fathers use part of the benefit.[4]
- *Subsidized childcare services.* Most Western European countries provide free, high-quality preschools for three- to five-year-olds, and many also subsidize childcare for infants and toddlers. An astounding 95 percent of three- to five-year-olds in France and Belgium are in childcare.[5]
- *Housing allowances.* Housing is a major cost for families. Housing allowances provide government cash assistance with housing costs, available to families with children whose income falls below a certain level. Despite the income test, housing allowances often reach far into the middle class—aiding one-third of families with children in Sweden and one-quarter in France. Further, they form part of a comprehensive housing policy, which includes public housing construction as well as subsidies for private construction.[6]
- *Universal, subsidized health care.* The United States is the only wealthy country that lacks a universal health care plan. In addition to guaranteed health care, some European countries, such as France, run special systems of preventive care for pregnant women and preschool children.[7]

This family policy package does not mean that life in Western Europe is paradise for families. There are still economic hardships, gender inequalities, and gaps in the safety net. But it does keep these societies far less stratified than the increasingly polarized United States, and provides families with a basic level of security and flexibility. As we saw in Chapter Six, government assistance lifts many more poor families out of poverty in Western Europe than in the United States. It allows European families to balance work and family in ways that are relatively sane and sensible. Is it merely a dream to wish for the same in the United States?

Family policies for the United States

The costs of real welfare reform are high—but so are the costs of poverty, child neglect, and overwork. Under the current system, low-income families, women, and children disproportionately bear these costs, yet that does not mean that the rest of society escapes them. Perhaps the most striking element of Europe's family policies is not any particular policy, but rather the deeply held philosophy of "social solidarity," meaning that "children and young people belong to the entire community, not just to their individual families," in the words of researcher Katherine McFate.[8] Here are eight broad policy approaches the United States should take that embody the notion of social solidarity.

1. Financially support full-time childcare

This means financially supporting women engaged in full-time childcare or providing alternate sources of childcare for those who work outside the home.

If we acknowledge the reality of children's needs and sincerely value families, then the important work of taking care of young children or relatives who cannot take care of themselves is, at times, best kept within the family. Even with childcare supports, families must be afforded the right to choose who does the work of childrearing. In short, jobs simply cannot be perceived as the answer for all single mothers at all times. For families with only one adult, this means that paid employment will not always be desirable or even possible, and will require some form of cash assistance.

What about parents who do choose paid employment? States currently provide childcare vouchers to women on welfare who are involved in employment and training programs, most often for up to one year after they get a job. One of the main reasons women return to welfare is that they can't make a job work for them, and the inability to find and pay for safe, quality daycare is a key barrier. But women who receive welfare are not the only people who need help securing childcare. *All* parents with children want to see their children cared for properly. Yet, for many families, working for pay and taking care of children is a costly proposition. The only comprehensive childcare program in the

United States today is a federal tax deduction, and it is inadequate. Covering only a small portion of childcare costs, it only benefits families who make enough to owe income taxes. Perhaps its largest drawback is that it does not increase the *supply* of childcare. This deduction is supplemented in a limited way by small block grant and subsidy programs, a tax exemption for children, and the Earned Income Credit (a refundable credit for families with at least one child). But all of this does not even come close to creating a childcare *system*. And it falls far short of what most European countries provide: universal, free childcare (at least for ages three to five), plus cash family allowances based on the number of children.

Families that include someone at home doing unpaid work all day long are vanishing quickly. Women realize that their economic independence rests on their ability to earn wages, and increasingly, two incomes are necessary to assure a reasonable standard of living. Indeed, it is just this fact that has made jobs the cornerstone of welfare reform. If we as a country expect many more women to work, however, we had better be prepared to pay for raising children.

2. Create more jobs—and stop assuming jobholders have a wife at home

In early 1997, in the midst of economic boom times by all standard business indicators, over seven million Americans were unemployed. Over two million had been unemployed for fifteen weeks or more. And these official unemployment numbers don't include those who have given up looking for work, or those who want full-time work but have only been able to find shorter hours. If we include these people, the number of unemployed swells to thirteen million. Though the Federal Reserve Board and economists in their ivory towers may define this situation as full employment, it most certainly is not. The federal government could do far more to create jobs, from targeting monetary policy toward higher employment goals and increasing economic development investments in depressed areas, to directly funding public service employment. Full employment is an old idea that still makes sense.

While many people who want to work can't find a job, others are overworked. Jobs that can support a family often require a full-time commitment (or more), leaving many people exhausted. It's not just the welfare system that has to come to terms with family needs; it's employers as well. With women making up 46 percent of the workforce—and men also taking on more childcare responsibilities—a change in work styles is overdue.

All workers, men and women, need more time and flexibility on a day-to-day, week-to-week basis. One way to provide everyone with more time is to move to a thirty-hour work week. Short of this, federal and state governments could do more to reward businesses that adopt family-friendly policies. Businesses clearly get benefits from such policies: a new study by Massachusetts Institute of Technology Management Professor Lotte Bailyn and others found that departments at Xerox who took work/family needs into account saw unprecedented reductions in absences, decreases in customer-response times, and on-schedule completions of new product development.[9] Unfortunately, many employers place more value on controlling their employees and squeezing out as many hours of labor as possible—and as long as this is true, public policy is needed to tip the balance the other way.

3. Boost wages to a "living wage" level, and make them fairer

With earnings the main source of income for most families and the key alternative to government support, we can't afford to leave so many adults stuck in low-wage employment. Between 1973 and 1996, the average hourly wage for nonsupervisory workers in the private sector slumped from $13.60 to $11.82 (in 1996 dollars).[10] For the lowest wage earners, even year-round, full-time work is no guarantee of avoiding poverty. Currently, 11 percent of poor families have a head who works full-time, year-round; 14 percent of year-round, full-time workers earn less than their family's poverty line.[11] And job discrimination against people of color, non-English speakers, and women persists, often lowering the wages of these groups.

There is no magic bullet that will solve the problems of low and unfair wage levels, but three measures could make a big difference. First, *mandate equal pay for comparable work.*

"Equal pay for equal work" is an important principle, but with women and men segregated into different types of jobs (with very different pay levels!), it does not do enough to overcome gender inequality within specific jobs. Comparable worth—that is, requiring equal pay for work requiring comparable, though not identical, skills, education, and responsibility—could do a lot more to close the gender pay gap. Economists Deborah Figart and June Lapidus estimated the effect of comparable worth, also called pay equity, on women's wages. They concluded that a comprehensive pay equity program would raise women's average hourly wage by 8.5 percent. The biggest effect would be seen at the bottom of the scale: before comparable worth, 25 percent of women would not earn enough to bring a family of three up to the poverty line; after comparable worth, only 15 percent would fall short of this threshold.[12] Poor women need pay equity most, but all women need it.

Second, *raise the minimum wage, and expand requirements for a living wage*. Almost 60 percent of minimum-wage workers are women. Further, women are more likely than men to stay in minimum-wage jobs over the course of their working lives. Between 1979 and 1995, the inflation-adjusted value of the minimum wage tumbled by 30 percent. In 1996, Congress increased the minimum wage from $4.25 an hour to $5.15, still leaving it far below its 1979 level of $6.18 (in 1996 dollars). Some point out that, even at that higher level, a minimum wage still would not be a living wage. A modest definition of a living wage is one that allows a full-time, year-round worker to bring a family of four up to its poverty threshold—$7.71 per hour in 1996. Community-labor coalitions have pressed city governments to require any business receiving city business or tax breaks to pay a living wage, and have recently won such laws in Baltimore, Los Angeles, Milwaukee, and Minneapolis. Figart and Lapidus estimated that bumping the minimum wage up from $4.25 to $4.75 would boost women's average wages by 2 to 4 percent.[13] An important complement to increasing the minimum wage is expanding the Earned Income Credit, a refundable federal income tax credit aimed at low-income families.

Third, *level the playing field for labor unions*. While the track record of unions on diversity remains mixed, the most dynamic unions today are ones aggressively recruiting and supporting women and people of color. Unions raise wages most for the lowest paid—good news for women and minority workers. Union representation increases a woman's wage by an average of 20 percent (over that of an otherwise identical woman without union coverage). Taking this into account, doubling the percentage of unionized women should push women's average wage 3 percent higher.[14] Every bit helps! But union coverage has shrunk from one-third of the workforce in the 1950s to less than one-sixth today. Businesses have discovered that they can run hardball union-busting campaigns—misleading, threatening, and even firing workers—and pay only minimal penalties, usually years after the damage is done. To level this playing field, we need stronger laws protecting workers' rights to unionize without fear of employer retaliation and to strike without fear of being immediately—and permanently—replaced.

4. Tame the family budget busters

Housing is the biggest expense for most families, and paying for health care is a serious problem for those who don't get coverage from an employer or the government. And the growth in both housing and health care costs is outrunning income, leaving increasing numbers of families without adequate shelter or coverage.

Housing costs have grown faster than income since the early 1980s, leading to declining home ownership and rising rent-to-income ratios. The housing squeeze pinches low-income households the hardest. Nearly one-fifth of all renters, but *one-half of low-income renters*, spend more than half of their income on housing costs.[15] Whereas in 1970 there were more low-rent units than low-income renters, by 1993 the situation had dramatically reversed, and there were 4.7 million fewer affordable units than low-income renters.[16] One predictable result has been growing homelessness: a careful 1992 estimate put the ranks of the homeless at 600,000 on any given night, and 1.2 million over the course of a year.[17] And families with children are the fastest-growing group among the homeless.

While a variety of approaches can help make housing more affordable, the best strategy is to combine approaches. Rent vouchers and opportunities for affordable home ownership can assist many families, but we also need public housing as a last resort. Low-income women—like any other group—have particular housing needs, and some nonprofit organizations have specifically targeted those needs. For example, the Women's Development Corporation (WDC) in Providence, Rhode Island, has developed 550 units of housing for low-income women. WDC places a priority on integrating women into a variety of networks in the broader community, "so that they see themselves as the same as others in the community, with the same rights," says Susan Aitcheson, codirector of the WDC. The Boston-based Women's Institute for Housing and Economic Development (WIHED), rather than developing housing itself, gives technical assistance to organizations providing housing for women and children. A partial list of WIHED projects highlights the diversity of women's housing situations, including grandmothers raising their grandchildren, Haitian-American single mothers and their children, teen mothers trying to make it on their own, recovering substance abusers (many of whom are trying to regain custody of their children), elderly women who have been homeless, and younger formerly homeless women and their children. Creative groups like WDC and WIHED deserve support.

Health care is the other major family budget buster. While the average family spent 18 percent of its income on health care in 1992, the burden weighs most heavily on the poorest one-fifth of the population, which shelled out 23 percent of its income for medical care. Thirty-nine million people lacked health insurance in 1992, but even among those who were insured, many reported that they had trouble paying for health care expenses: even among people with private health insurance, one in six reported difficulty paying medical bills.[18]

After all the sound and fury over health care reform in the last few years, the only federal reform in place so far is to guarantee people the right to continue health insurance coverage at their own expense after leaving a job. It is past time to get in step with the rest of the industrialized world and make health care a basic right. The other industrialized countries, which provide universal coverage through "single-payer" plans (meaning that there is a single, government-controlled insurer for all), deliver health care more cheaply than the United States *and* have healthier populations.[19]

5. *Expand the safety net*

Neither welfare recipients nor the general public is enthusiastic about welfare—to put it mildly. But cash assistance—whether as TANF or the state-structured AFDC programs—remains necessary as the ultimate safety net for families with children. Yet expanding other parts of the social safety net could help to reduce reliance on welfare. Two candidates for expansion are unemployment insurance and temporary disability insurance.

Unemployment insurance (UI), established as part of the 1935 Social Security Act, offers compensation to unemployed workers based on their earnings while employed. Research by the Washington-based Institute for Women's Policy Research indicates, however, that UI is currently a fairly exclusive program.[20] This is true even for men and full-time workers, the traditional beneficiaries of the program: 74 percent of unemployed men, and 62 percent of unemployed full-time workers, do not meet eligibility requirements—including the reasons for leaving a job, number of weeks worked, minimum pay levels, and industry restrictions. But women and part-time workers are most often shut out: 80 percent of unemployed women, and 90 percent of unemployed part-time workers, fail to meet eligibility criteria for UI. The percentage of the unemployed who receive UI has declined significantly for several reasons: women and part-time workers now make up a larger share of the workforce; unemployment durations have lengthened, so more unemployed people reach UI's time limits; and states have simply tightened eligibility rules. And although many welfare recipients cycle between welfare and work, only 11 percent of working welfare mothers draw on UI—relying instead on welfare as a "poor woman's unemployment insurance."

What can be done? The Center for Law and Social Policy has suggested a variety of reforms that would enable UI to help more people: widen eligibility, extend time limits, add a component covering temporary disability (including pregnancy and childbirth), and possibly even consolidate the UI program with cash assistance for families with children that include an employable adult.[21]

Another option would be to strengthen and expand temporary disability insurance (TDI) systems. About one-quarter of women who leave their jobs do so because of family reasons, such as pregnancy. The 1993 Family and Medical Leave Act (FMLA) guarantees twelve weeks of unpaid leave for childbirth and family illnesses or other emergencies. This helps, but the FMLA only covers about half of the workforce (those in businesses employing fifty people or more), and a mere 2 to 4 percent of workers eligible for time off actually take leaves.[22] After all, few people can afford to take unpaid time off. Creating universal, paid family leave, as in all Western European countries, would do far more to ease work-family tensions. This could be done by establishing a nationwide temporary disability insurance program—or simply by strengthening the FMLA. Five states (California, Hawaii, New Jersey, New York, and Rhode Island) currently operate temporary disability insurance systems—in effect, replacing the current unpaid Family and Medical Leave Act with paid leave.[23] The programs offer partial wage replacement —starting at about 50 percent of pay and capping at a specified maximum—for personal medical disability (including pregnancy).[24] State TDI systems could be extended to provide paid leave for women and men who need to suspend work in order to take care of sick family members. The Institute for Women's Policy Research estimated the monthly total cost per worker in ten states for current (or proposed) TDI benefits plus paid family leave for care of a sick spouse, elderly parents, sick children, or newborns. The costs ranged from $17.70 per month in New Jersey to $12.60 in Rhode Island—hardly a budget buster.[25] Costs could be shared by employers, employees, and/or the government—since all have much to gain from such a program.

6. Provide affordable and available education and training for all

The United States boasts one of the best higher-education systems in the world. But the U.S. education and training system stacks up far worse for the 75 percent of the workforce with less than a four-year college degree, and worst of all for those who do not finish high school. Since the large majority of welfare recipients have no more than a high school diploma, they suffer from these shortcomings in the country's school-and-skill system—but so do many other groups: displaced workers, older women re-entering the workforce, and young people who don't follow the college track. And as the tuition costs of postsecondary education mount, the simple affordability of college has also become an issue.

The education and training system must be rebuilt from the bottom up. High school students in noncollege tracks need a curriculum that is richer and more closely linked to actual jobs —possibly adapting Western European apprenticeship programs. The "second-chance" system for those who drop out of high school or who require retraining must be expanded and retooled. Currently, publicly subsidized second-chance training is largely limited to people who are persistently poor and unemployed; in many employers' eyes, it is a stigma rather than a credential. An improved second-chance training system would take in a much wider spectrum of people, recognizing that most, if not all, of the workforce needs retraining at some point. It would offer special supports, rather than segregation, for those with greater training needs. Over the last ten years, for every $100 of production taking place in the United States, the government spent 10¢ on training; the rate in Sweden was six times as great.[26]

Both secondary education as well as second-chance education and training must strike a balance: they must provide work-relevant knowledge, often imparted in a work setting, but they must also help people develop broad understanding and critical thinking that go beyond narrow job-specific skills. Without the second component, workers can remain trapped in low-level jobs or be stranded when jobs disappear. A useful model in this regard is the new vocational education goal of studying "all aspects of an industry," including financial and social as well as technical ones.

Public sector education and training can only fill part of the gap. By international standards, U.S. firms themselves do not provide enough training for workers. When Bill Clinton ran for president in 1992, he proposed a payroll tax of 1 to 1.5 percent to fund a pool that employers could draw on to provide training to their workforces. And while nothing ever came of that campaign promise, such an incentive to train makes good sense.

Finally, we need to broaden access to and affordability of higher education. The combination of skyrocketing tuition plus a college requirement for a growing number of jobs adds up to a crisis. President Clinton's $1,500 tax break for college tuition does little to help. It is small, and aids poor families least, since they often do not pay enough taxes to benefit from the break. One step toward a more complete solution is expanded student aid, including aid tied to national service and loans whose repayment schedules would depend on actual postcollege earnings. Another part of the solution is bolstering public higher education, which—although in crisis across much of the country—continues to offer the best bargain in postsecondary schooling.

7. Promote community-based economic development

Private sector-driven development has left increasing numbers of people—and in some cases, entire neighborhoods or regions—stranded. And mistrust of government is at an all-time high. While government action is needed to set standards and redistribute resources, there is a third option: community-based economic development, in which locally controlled nonprofits take the lead in providing employment opportunities, housing, training, and services.

Community economic development can take a wide variety of forms, such as supporting the creation of small businesses and producer cooperatives, investing in the revitalization of neighborhood commercial areas, or training community members for better jobs. Some community economic development organizations, such as Chicago's Women's Self-Employment Project or Los Angeles's Coalition of Women's Economic Development, focus specifically on women. The strengths of community control are the flexibility, creativity, and accountability that it brings, plus the fact that community action on economic development helps to build broader social and political cohesion. On the downside, even when a poor community pools its resources, those resources are still quite limited—and communities acting separately can do little to change the large structural forces and the market economy's "rules of the game" that powerfully shape their destinies. Despite these limitations, community-based strategies have made an important difference in many areas and deserve government support.

8. Secure funding with a fairer tax structure

Let's face up to the fact that wage earnings and child support from absent fathers are not going be enough to pull single-mother families out of poverty. Some supplemental assistance in the form of child allowances, childcare subsidies, and transfers will be necessary to help bear the costs of childrearing. The best way to share those costs is through government financing. Since the government gets its income from taxes and fees, financing new government programs means raising taxes or cutting spending on other areas.

It may not seem politically and economically feasible to finance new programs when states are strapped for cash and the federal government is concerned with reducing its already large deficit. But the costs of our current system are already unacceptably high. Women, children, and people of color disproportionately bear the costs of child poverty and all its attendant problems. Refusing to fund the programs recommended here may be far more costly.

To finance new programs, the United States needs a fairer tax system at the federal and state levels. This means overhauling the current tax structure so that those who can most afford to pay taxes do so. In the 1980s, the federal government cut taxes for the wealthiest, placing a larger share of the burden on middle- and low-income families. These changes, plus large increases in employee Social Security contributions, have reduced federal tax receipts *and* made lower-income families pay a higher percentage of their income to fund programs they typically do not get to take part in. Recent tax reforms have helped to correct some of the plunder of the 1980s, but there is still a long way to go at the federal level. In the states and localities, taxes are even less fair: states, for instance, rely heavily on property and sales taxes, which take a bigger chunk, percentagewise, out of low incomes than high ones. After federal tax deductions, total state and local taxes in 1995 claimed a nationwide average of 12 percent from the incomes of the poorest fifth of families of four, but only 6 percent from the incomes of the richest 1 percent.[27] Graduated state income taxes—tax rates based on the ability to pay, as at the federal level—would be a real step forward.

Surveys show that U.S. citizens would be willing to pay more taxes if the money went to fund policies they believe in. The programs proposed here have important economic and social benefits for everyone. To start with, providing an enhanced sense of economic security in the form of a social floor, for every U.S. citizen—including the rights to health care, childcare, a child allowance, and housing—is likely to improve the productivity of American workers immensely. During and after World War II, American workers' productivity on the job increased because the private and public sectors both offered stronger guarantees of economic well-being. The programs recommended here are also sure to reduce workplace absenteeism, as family-friendly policies at Xerox and other companies have already done. Finally, and most important, these programs will bolster a sense of shared values and commitment in society about the work of raising *all* our children, sending the message: the work of raising and caring for children is important enough to be a social responsibility, not just an individual one.

Replacing contradictions with consistencies

Before turning to political strategy in the next chapter, we can succinctly restate the agenda for women's economic equality by revisiting the four contradictions discussed in Chapter One: First, we are a country that says we should value families, and above all else children, yet we devalue the *work* of taking care of children. Second, we are a country that expects all able-bodied adults to be in the labor force, yet we leave job creation to a private sector unable to provide a job to everyone who wants one. Third, as a country, we firmly believe that a job is the best way out of poverty, but we have allowed increasing numbers of jobs to slip below a living wage level—even as businesses cut back on essential fringe benefits, such as health insurance. Finally, financial dependency within the family is considered natural, as when a woman stays home to cook, clean, and care for her children. But when she does not have a husband and wants to do exactly the same kind of necessary work in her home, dependency on the government is deplored.

These four contradictions put all women—but especially single mothers—in a no-win situation. If a woman does paid work, she is not taking care of her family. If she is taking care of her family, she is not living up to her obligations to do paid work. And while Murphy Brown may have beaten Dan Quayle in the battle over family values, Quayle and other conservatives are winning the war by blaming women for the problems of insufficient time and money to take care of our families and communities. The right wing has effectively blamed women's rights for problems that are actually caused by a deadly combination of a market system that fails to provide jobs with living wages and a political and economic system that refuses to socialize the cost of raising children. Welfare recipients are cannon fodder in this battle.

Women's economic equality can only be won by completing a broad reform agenda that demands that this country divide up economic resources in a very different, more just way than currently allocated. Only by resolving the contradictions of our current situation—and creating new *consistencies* in values and action—will we overcome the glass ceilings and the bottomless pits that face women today.

The major policies proposed in this book—including real welfare reform, universal childcare and support, comparable worth, and a job structure that can provide livable wages and adequate nonwork time for all this country's adults—would go a long way toward resolving the inconsistencies in our current economic system. But proposing better policies is the easy part. The hard part is gaining support for such policies in these angry and fearful times.

Notes

1. The framework for this summary draws on Sheila B. Kamerman and Alfred J. Kahn, "Family Policy: Has the United States Learned from Europe?" *Policy Studies Review*, vol. 8, no. 3 (1989): 581-98. Other useful overviews include: Gosta Esping-Anderson, "The Equality-Employment Trade-Off: Europe's Welfare States at the End of the Century," mimeo, University of Trento and Instituto Juan March, 1995; Karen Gibson and Peter Hall, "American Poverty and Social Policy: What Can Be Learned from the European Experience," Social Science Research Council, New York (distributed by the National Center for Children in Poverty, Columbia University, New York), 1993; Jane Lewis, ed., *Women and Social Policies in Europe: Work, Family, and the State* (Aldershot, England: Edward Elgar, 1993); Katherine McFate, Roger Lawson, and William Julius Wilson, eds., *Poverty, Inequality and the Future of Social Policy: Western States in the New World Order* (New York: Russell Sage, 1995).
2. Barbara Bergmann, "The French Child Welfare System: An Excellent System We Could Adapt and Afford," in *Sociology and the Public*

Agenda, ed. William Julius Wilson (Newbury Park, CA: Sage Publications, 1993).

3. Lee Rainwater and Timothy Smeeding, "U.S. Doing Poorly—Compared to Others," *National Center for Children in Poverty—News and Issues* (fall/winter 1995).

4. Kamerman and Kahn, op. cit.; Søren Carlsen and Jørgen Larsen, eds., *The Equality Dilemma: Reconciling Working Life and Family Life, Viewed in an Equality Perspective—The Danish Example* (Copenhagen: The Danish Equal Status Council, 1994), figure 14a; Linda Haas, *Equal Parenthood and Social Policy: A Study of Parental Leave in Sweden* (Albany: State University of New York Press, 1992); Raju Narisetti and Rochelle Sharpe, "Take It or Leave It, Norway Tells New Fathers," *Wall Street Journal*, 29 August 1995, p. A1.

5. Kamerman and Kahn, op. cit.; Carlsen and Larsen, op. cit., table 14.b; Sheila Kamerman, "Child Care Policies and Programs: An International Overview," *Journal of Social Issues*, vol. 47, no. 2 (1991).

6. Kamerman and Kahn, op. cit.; Gibson and Hall, op. cit.

7. Bergmann, op. cit.

8. Katherine McFate, *Poverty, Inequality, and the Crisis of Social Policy: Summary of Findings* (Washington, D.C.: Joint Center for Political and Economic Studies, 1991), p. 23.

9. Sue Shellenbarger, "Family-Friendly Jobs Are the First Step to Efficient Workplace," *Wall Street Journal*, 15 May 1996, p. B1.

10. U.S. Council of Economic Advisors, *Economic Report of the President* (Washington, D.C.: Government Printing Office, 1997), table B-45.

11. Computed by authors from U.S. Bureau of the Census, Current Population Survey, March 1994, computer tape.

12. Deborah M. Figart and June Lapidus, "A Gender Analysis of U.S. Labor Market Policies for the Working Poor," *Feminist Economics*, vol. 1, no. 3 (1995).

13. Ibid.

14. Calculated by the authors based on the union wage premium of 20 percent (Lawrence Mishel and Jared Bernstein, eds., *The State of Working America 1994-95* [Armonk, NY: M.E. Sharpe, 1994]), and women's 1995 union representation rate of 14 percent (U.S. Bureau of Labor Statistics, *Employment and Earnings*, January 1996, table 40).

15. Peter Dreier and John Atlas, "U.S. Housing Policy at the Crossroads: A Progressive Agenda to Rebuild the Housing Constituency," Working Paper, Occidental College, International and Public Affairs Center, Los Angeles, 1996.

16. Edward B. Lazere, *In Short Supply: The Growing Affordable Housing Gap* (Washington, D.C.: Center on Budget and Policy Priorities, 1995).

17. Martha Burt, *Over the Edge: The Growth of Homelessness in the 1980s* (New York: Russell Sage Foundation, 1992).

18. Information in this paragraph is from Edith Rassell, "Health Care: Expenditures Exceed Results," in *The State of Working America 1994-95*,

eds. Lawrence Mishel and Jared Bernstein (Armonk, NY: M.E. Sharpe, 1994).

19. Ibid. For example, despite lower average income levels, many industrialized countries have lower infant mortality and longer life expectancy than the United States.

20. Institute for Women's Policy Research, "Unemployment Insurance: Barriers to Access for Women and Part-time Workers," Research-in-brief, Washington, D.C., 1995; Roberta Spalter-Roth, Heidi Hartmann, and Beverly Burr, "IncoMe Insecurity: The Failure of Unemployment Insurance to Reach Out to Working AFDC Mothers," Institute for Women's Policy Research, presented at the Second Annual Employment Task Force Conference, March 20-22, 1994.

21. Steve Savner and Mark Greenberg, "Reforming the Unemployment Insurance System to Better Meet the Needs of Low-income Families," revised draft, Center for Law and Social Policy, Washington, D.C., March 1996.

22. Glenn Burkins, "Family Leave: A Government Survey Shows Few Are Making Use of It," *Wall Street Journal*, 26 March 1996, p. A1.

23. Institute for Women's Policy Research, "Using Temporary Disability Insurance to Provide Paid Family Leave: A Comparison with the Family and Medical Leave Act," Research-in-brief, Washington, D.C., 1995.

24. Kirsten Wever, *The Family and Medical Leave Act: Assessing Temporary Wage Replacement for Family and Medical Leave* (Cambridge, MA: Radcliffe Public Policy Institute, 1996).

25. Institute for Women's Policy Research, "Using Temporary Disability Insurance to Provide Paid Family Leave: A Comparison with the Family and Medical Leave Act," Research-in-brief, Washington, D.C., 1995

26. Karen Gibson and Peter Hall, "American Poverty and Social Policy: What Can Be Learned from the European Experience," Social Science Research Council, New York (distributed by the National Center for Children in Poverty, Columbia University, New York), 1993.

27. Citizens for Tax Justice, *Who Pays: A Distributional Analysis of the Tax System in All 50 States* (Washington, D.C.: Citizens for Tax Justice, 1996).

10

The Power to Win Women's Economic Equality

While women's economic advancement over the last forty years has been tremendous, the agenda of equal opportunity remains unfinished. While it is easier for a woman to get elected to office, hold a full-time job, or support herself without having to depend on a man, women still face enormous barriers to economic equality. For some educated and accomplished women, that barrier is the glass ceiling; for far too many women—and their children—the barrier is a bottomless pit, with few ladders up and out.

Fulfilling an agenda for women's economic equality will take more than debunking myths, explaining realities, and proposing new policies, however sensible they may be. Achieving equality is a question of power—of economic and social power, but most decisively of political power. At this point, the power of low-income women and their allies is at a low ebb, but advocates of equality have begun to form new alliances and hatch new strategies. The coming years may see some surprising power shifts.

Power surge: What it will take to reverse economic inequality

There is no easy answer for how to repulse the backlash against welfare and women's rights. But from the long history of struggles for economic and social equality in this country—from the setbacks as well as the triumphs—we can outline the elements of a strategy for change.[1] We focus here particularly on a strategy for winning real welfare reform that can actually help end poverty and enhance economic equality for all women. That's because we believe that the best way to achieve economic equality for all women is by lifting up those at the bottom.

To build the power to advance women's economic equality, we need a strategy with the following four components:[2] First, the strategy must target *power in the workplace*—expanding the voice and bargaining power of women and low-wage workers in the employment relationship. Another key element is *conventional politics*, encompassing electoral mobilization, lobbying, and litigation (challenging bad laws or the failure to implement good laws). Third, the *power of protest*, which has always been important for "outsiders" far from the centers of power, remains essential. Finally, the ultimate battle involves *shaping public opinion*, by telling the truth in ways that spark people's imagination, sympathy, and solidarity.

A key theme that runs through all four factors is recognizing and confronting the differences among women. Women remain divided by race and class; the glass ceiling is *not* equivalent to the bottomless pit. But as we have pointed out repeatedly, reduced rights for the poorest women undermine the rights and opportunities of all women—and ultimately, of most men as well, since the "work vs. family" conflict increasingly traps them, too. The challenge is to build coalitions across race, class, and gender lines.

The four strategic elements of workplace power, conventional politics, protest, and public opinion are by no means separate. Changing laws via conventional politics can widen the scope for power in the workplace or for protest. Protest is a tool for influencing workplace power, conventional politics, and public opinion. Public opinion, in turn, exerts enormous leverage on legislative action and on the effectiveness of protest. But it is helpful to view the four as distinct, though overlapping and interacting, arenas of action. Through this prism, let's look briefly at the past, present, and possible future battles for women's economic equality.

Workplace power struggles

If we are to become a "nation of workers" that includes even mothers of young children, then the struggle for workplace equality is a vital component for improving the lives of women and their families. The history of workplace-based efforts to win equality for women is largely, for better or worse, the history of unions. As social historian Ruth Milkman points out, there have been four major cohorts of unionism in the United States, and each cohort's attitude toward women at its inception has continued to color its relationship toward women.[3] Dating back to the 19th century, the earliest stable unions were male-dominated craft unions, such as those in the building trades and printing, which historically viewed women with suspicion as low-wage competitors—and to a large extent continue to do so. (Other union movements from that era, such as the Knights of Labor and later the International Workers of the World, welcomed women, but did not survive as mass movements.) A second wave of unionism in the 1910s, especially in the clothing and textile industries, sought to organize women—who made up a growing portion of the workforce in these industries—but maintained a paternalistic attitude toward them as vulnerable workers in need of particular protection. The reality was more complicated than this attitude allowed: women were especially subject to employer abuse in the early decades of the century, but also led and took part in militant actions, such as the 1909 "Uprising of the 20,000," a hard-fought thirteen-week strike of women shirtwaist workers in New York City.

In the 1930s, the tide turned for women in the labor movement with the organizing of industrial unions by the Congress of Industrial Organizations (CIO). Women were integral to the mass-production manufacturing industries in the 1930s and 1940s. The CIO organized them as equals and took a formal stand against gender discrimination—although CIO unions also took part in the displacement of women workers by returning servicemen at the end of World War II. Finally, the service, clerical, and public sector unions that grew after the war have organized occupations that are predominantly female (nurses, teachers, and clerical workers), and have been powerfully influenced by the resurgent women's movement that emerged in the 1960s.

Unions from this wave—such as the Service Employees International Union (SEIU), the American Federation of State, County, and Municipal Employees (AFSCME), the American Nurses Association (ANA), and the National Education Association (NEA)—have promoted women leaders, and SEIU and AFSCME actively campaigned for comparable worth beginning in the 1980s.

The present state of workplace efforts for gender equality reflects this mixed legacy. At one extreme, women in the building trades continue to battle against outright exclusion (carried out through informal means, since formal bars are now illegal). On the other hand, "fourth-wave" unions representing service and clerical workers are actively seeking to organize women, win pay equity, and establish more work/family flexibility. Enriching the mix is the emergence, beginning in the 1970s, of new advocacy groups oriented toward women workers, but not directly focused on unionization. Cleveland-based Nine to Five/National Association of Working Women is perhaps the best known, but numerous other groups—such as Boston's Office Technology Education Project and San Francisco's New Ways to Work—combine education, lobbying, and in some cases, organizing to confront issues ranging from workplace safety and health to pay equity and work/family issues. Meanwhile, within the AFL-CIO itself, new leadership elected in 1995 rode into office on a reform platform. After a century of federation presidents from unions representing male, blue-collar workers (particularly the building trades), the AFL-CIO elected John Sweeney, then president of SEIU—a fast-growing, forward-looking fourth-wave union that mainly encompasses white- and pink-collar workers. Sweeney's slate included Linda Chavez-Thompson of AFSCME as executive vice president—another fourth waver and the first woman to hold a top AFL-CIO office. It's too early to assess the performance of these new union leaders, but at least they offer the promise of new kinds of activism. At this point, the main obstacle to union participation in fighting for equality for women is no longer hostility or indifference within the labor movement (though those problems certainly remain), but rather organized labor's shrinking share of the workforce, which continues to dwindle.

And that sets the stage for the future. In our view—and in the view of many innovators in the labor movement—the strategies most likely to succeed in rebuilding the labor movement are those that increase their involvement in battles for gender equality. Women make up a growing share of the workforce, particularly in the barely unionized service sector, and are, on average, more supportive of unions than men. Any survival strategy for the AFL-CIO must place a priority on organizing predominantly female occupations and industries. More broadly, in order to succeed, the union movement must reclaim its mantle as the advocate for all workers and low-income people, not just the few covered by a union contract. From Sweeney down to the local level, much of the labor movement has begun to take on this challenge, championing a higher minimum wage, local living wage ordinances, and other measures that will help the lowest paid. Though they have not made welfare reform a central issue, the AFL-CIO leadership has taken some progressive stands opposing punitive reform—in part, due to the displacement threat that workfare poses to their public employee membership base —and local leaders have, in some cases, been active participants in coalitions defending welfare rights.[4]

In addition, the labor movement of the future is likely to make more use of organizing tools that offer new opportunities to mobilize women. Because labor law itself affords little protection for unions, they will have to rely increasingly on labor-community coalitions. Women have long played a prominent role in community-based organizations, and community action often focuses on "consumption" issues of particular concern to women as mothers and homemakers: housing, health care, social services, and so on. In building bridges with communities, unions will be compelled to take on more of this agenda. Unions will also have to undertake more city-wide, industry-wide organizing —like the Justice for Janitors campaign, which has tried to organize janitors across whole cities—rather than traditional shop-by-shop campaigns. Again, since family responsibilities and limited job opportunities make women more likely than men to move in and out of the workforce and from one workplace to another, this new organizing approach should be a better fit with women's work lives.

New organizing strategies will be critical in expanding the workplace power of women and all workers. But what's needed is not just more organizing. Unions must find ways to overcome their isolation from most American workers. They must rebuild the public perception that they stand for all working people, particularly the most vulnerable. They must carve out a political stance distinct from that of the Democratic Party, which is increasingly, like the Republicans, a party run by and for the wealthy. Unions must pursue legislative influence to win reform of labor laws that level the organizing playing field, and to win laws assuring equal opportunity and a stronger social safety net. In short, they must work to introduce issues of class into conventional politics—the arena to which we now turn.

Conventional politics: Unconventional approaches?

In some ways, conventional politics has been the "toughest nut to crack" for low-income women and their advocates. Low representation of women in the political establishment and politicians' lack of interest in hearing from poor women have served to ice out calls for effective anti-poverty, employment, and childcare policies for women and their children. After all, children can't vote, and low-income people usually turn out at the polls only when candidates are addressing their issues—which occurs too infrequently.

Historically, women were largely locked out of conventional political activity, but hammered at the door until they got in. Women's suffrage organizations blossomed after the Civil War as part of a broader female-led movement for social improvement, finally winning the national vote for women in 1920. Even without the vote, the late 19th and early 20th centuries saw middle-class organizations such as the Women's Christian Temperance Union, the General Federation of Women's Clubs, and the National Association of Colored Women combine lobbying with education, charitable work, and in some cases, protest. Once the vote was won, the enormous, but superficially united, women's suffrage movement splintered: the National Woman Party proposed an Equal Rights Amendment in 1923 and pursued it single-mindedly, whereas the League of Women Voters and other women's organizations opposed the amendment on the basis that it would outlaw special protections for women workers, who were particularly vulnerable.[5] Nonetheless, women had

Table 10.1   Not a Representative Sample

The percentage of women elected officials, 1975 and 1995

Elected officeholders	Percentage of women 1975	1995
Members of Congress	4%	11%
Statewide elected officials	10	26
State legislators	8	21
Mayors*	5	18

*Mayors of cities with populations over 30,000.

Source: Cynthia Costello and Barbara Kivimae Krimgold, eds., *The American Woman*, 1996-97 (New York: W.W. Norton, 1996), table 6-3.

found their foothold and participated in political campaigns and coalitions from the New Deal of the 1930s to the Great Society and civil rights movements of the 1960s.

With the second women's movement of the 1960s came a new growth of women's lobbying and electoral organizations—such as the National Organization for Women and the National Women's Political Caucus—and a surge in the number of women elected officials, including, for the first time, governors and senators. Despite this, the Equal Rights Amendment fell short of ratification in 1982, and electoral progress has been limited. As Table 10.1 demonstrates, women are still underrepresented as elected officials at virtually all levels, especially in Congress.

One reason for this weakness is the frequent segregation of gender issues from those of class and race. On the one hand, organizations focusing on class (such as unions and community groups) and those focusing on race (civil rights groups and other organizations of people of color) have often relegated women's concerns to the second rank. On the other hand, the most prominent organizations of the second-wave women's movement have been led by white, professional women. The women's movement has most visibly and vigorously pursued issues of particular concern to middle-class women: access to professional jobs, availability of contraception and abortion, and equality in college curricula and athletics. This lopsided emphasis should not surprise us. Middle-class women are more likely than their poor and working-class sisters to have the time, money, and skills to build and lead organizations. So their influence on the movement is out of proportion to their numbers.

Furthermore, although the New Left ushered in the second wave of women's organizing, the New Right has also been effective at mobilizing women's political involvement around conservative backlash issues—opposition to abortion, defense of "traditional" family structures and white privilege, and support for tax cuts. Conservative women claim that not only has equality for women been accomplished, it has tipped the scales too far. Over the last two decades, this conservative backlash has channeled much of middle-class women's political energy into defending reproductive rights—including supporting prochoice candidates, regardless of their positions on women's economic equality.

Of course, sections of the women's movement have always emphasized building bridges across the divides of race and class. The reproductive rights movement illustrates the divergent strategies within the women's movement. From the 1970s onward, some coalitions—such as the National Abortion Rights Action League—focused narrowly on abortion rights, primarily mobilizing white, middle-class women. But other groups, such as those aggregated in the Reproductive Rights National Network, broadened the discussion to include opposition to forced contraception and sterilization—issues of particular concern to poor women—consciously striving to build a multiracial coalition. Even so, race- and class-conscious feminism remains a relatively small stream in an embattled movement. Its impact via conventional politics and even protest (as we shall see below) remains modest.

And that's where we stand today—with unprecedented numbers of women involved in conventional politics, but with the legislative agenda for women's equality largely stalled. The most visible woman governor, Christine Todd Whitman of New Jersey, is a tax-cutting, service-slashing conservative. And in 1995, when the harsh, Republican-crafted Personal Responsibility Act first came up for a vote, all five white women senators—Democrat and Republican alike—voted in favor of this welfare "reform." In

1996, when a modified version of the act passed after an added year of debate, three of these women switched to vote against it, but two (Kassenbaum and Mikulski) supported it once more. (The lone African-American woman in the Senate, Carol Moseley Braun, cast a nay vote both times.)

In fact, given the rush by state legislatures and governors to make welfare stingier, welfare advocates have had to rely primarily on the courts to defend welfare rights. Sitting judges still, to some extent, reflect the more liberal politics of earlier decades—and also take more seriously the constitutional and statutory guarantees that are often ignored by legislators and administrators anxious to cut costs and score political points. But litigation to defend the rights of poor women is only a holding action.

Regaining ground for women's equality in conventional politics calls for a four-pronged strategy. First, shifting the balance of power will require registering and mobilizing many who currently do not vote, particularly poor people and people of color. Second, any electoral advances will be limited until we reform campaign financing to lessen the influence of rich individuals and corporations. Not surprisingly, corporations and the wealthy have little interest in shifting funding priorities or in empowering low-income people. Progressive candidates who advocate for the type of policies discussed in the previous two chapters rarely can afford to make their way through the electoral process. Third, women in general, and low-income women in particular, need to consolidate new alliances in the electoral arena. Potential allies include the labor movement (as noted above), communities of color, and religious activists, who have often taken a strongly compassionate stand on issues of poverty and human services, despite some anti-woman positions on issues such as reproductive choice. One possible outcome of the alliance-building process is the growth of third parties, and the progress of new third party initiatives—such as the New Party, the Labor Party, and the 21st Century Party, initiated by the National Organization for Women—bears watching. Finally, new ways must be found to win over the hearts and minds of working people, so many of whom are currently swayed by their own economic anxiety to support anti-tax, anti-government, and anti-welfare policies.

Protest and survive

Protest has long been a forceful political lever for women, particularly for those who are poor.[6] The history of protest overlaps intimately with the history of unionism and electoral politics: unionists organized and struck, but also demonstrated for causes such as the eight-hour day; suffragists lobbied, but also rallied and marched. Women and their allies also have a long history of protests focused on issues of family, consumption, and unpaid domestic labor—issues that are typically more peripheral to unions and electoral politics. In the first years of the century, women repeatedly organized food boycotts and tenant unions to resist high prices and rents. During the 1920s, women's auxiliaries consisting of the wives of male union members demanded government creation of local health departments as well as maternal and child health programs. The Communist Party-organized United Council of Working Class Wives mobilized women on issues of cost of living, education, and social welfare, and when the Great Depression hit, joined the newly formed Unemployed Councils in demanding better relief along with more jobs. The Black Housewives' Leagues launched "Don't Buy Where You Can't Work" boycott campaigns in major cities, and also called for job creation during the Depression.

In the decades after World War II, the civil rights movement and the second-wave women's movement cross-fertilized with community organizing, giving rise to new protests. Civil rights activists, realizing that formal legal rights did not guarantee economic equality, broadened their focus once the Civil Rights Act was won in 1964. When Martin Luther King, Jr., was assassinated in 1967, he was in Memphis to support a sanitation workers' strike. The Johnson administration's mid-1960s War on Poverty offered an opening for a new wave of organizing in low-income communities. One dramatic outgrowth of this ferment was the National Welfare Rights Organization (NWRO), formed in 1967 by building on earlier local efforts. NWRO protested and lobbied to expand welfare recipients' rights, as well as activated poor women to demand AFDC benefits they were already entitled to but were not receiving. NWRO reached its high-water mark in 1971, with 900 chapters in fifty states, but folded in 1975 as political times changed.

In 1987, the newly formed National Welfare Rights Union (NWRU) picked up NWRO's torch; in 1992, the Oakland, California-based Women's Economic Agenda Project brought hundreds of women together for a Poor Women's Convention. Advocates for more effective welfare policies have devised creative approaches to protest. NWRU has organized welfare office sit-ins and takeovers of abandoned housing. On Valentine's Day 1995, in response to a call by JEDI Women (Justice, Economic Dignity, and Independence for Women) of Salt Lake City, activists in seventy-six cities carried out actions on the theme "Our Children's Hearts Are in Your Hands," targeting the punitive Personal Responsibility Act then before Congress. Participants in the actions mailed 61,000 postcards to legislators. The JEDI Women themselves marched into the Salt Lake City federal building to present their legislators with a port-a-crib full of cards colored by children in daycare centers.[7]

Advocates, welfare recipients, and their supporters have vigorously protested the implementation of the harsh Personal Responsibility and Work Opportunity Act that Congress finally passed in 1996. Since the act shifts enormous discretion over welfare to the state level, protest actions have particularly targeted state governments. For instance, Philadelphia's Kensington Welfare Rights Union and a wide range of other allies rallied in March 1997 to protest Pennsylvania's new welfare plan. Proposing an "Agreement of MUTUAL Responsibility" that called on Pennsylvania to provide jobs at a livable wage for all who need them, protestors marched outside a state office building and then occupied a local jobs center.[8] Similar actions are being repeated across the fifty states.

Unfortunately, in the shadow of conservative backlash, protests appear less and less effective, and are more likely to mobilize hundreds than tens of thousands in a given city. Ironically, women and men have turned out by the hundreds of thousands to defend other rights related to gender equity—reproductive choice, gay and lesbian rights—but have not responded in large numbers to the welfare "reform" that poses perhaps the sharpest current attack on women's rights. As in the case of conventional politics, protest strategies remain divided by race and class. Feminists have not succeeded in building—and in some cases, have not tried to build—on the long legacy of protest by poor and working-class women of diverse racial and ethnic groups. And the most powerful protests against racism and growing class inequality, from Solidarity Day in the 1980s to the Million Man March in the 1990s, have downplayed or ignored social and economic justice for women. Looking to the future, the prospects for truly effective protest remain dim unless we can begin to transcend these barriers.

However short protest may fall of its true potential, it continues to play two important roles in the push for welfare rights and full equality for women. For one thing, protests bring a visible moral element to political debates that can help to shape public opinion and shame legislators. Though protests may not currently seem to move us much farther forward on welfare rights, they are most definitely helping to prevent us from sliding farther backwards! But protests serve a second role as well, one where there is room for growth and experimentation: they make an unfair system harder to govern. The National Welfare Rights Organization strategy started by mobilizing poor women to demand enforcement of rights that were already on the books, exploiting the margin of administrative discretion that existed; they backed up these demands with the threat of civil disruption. We can't apply the same strategy uncritically at a time of cutbacks, but we can apply the same principles. For example, in many states, the executive branch is using administrative discretion to reduce eligibility and benefit levels *beyond* what's required by law, so they can boast of reduced welfare rolls and decreased spending. These discretionary actions mark a pressure point where protest can potentially win immediate, material gains for poor women, while exposing politicians' dishonesty. In many cases, social services staff, whose own jobs are threatened by the anti-welfare assault, may be helpful in identifying and acting on these pressure points.

The battle for public opinion

History teaches us that mobilizing to shape public opinion has often been a two-edged sword. For instance, middle-class female reformers used arguments about morality and the sacredness of the family to win support for Mother's Aid, the state-level predecessor to AFDC. But those same arguments, coupled with class prejudice, convinced the reformers and their allies that Mother's Aid should involve close monitoring of the behavior of recipients, and should only be made available to "morally fit" mothers.[9] As this example points out, U.S. public opinion—and with it U.S. public policy—has long distinguished between the deserving and undeserving poor.[10]

That distinction still haunts us today. Sympathy for poor people, especially children, coexists with resentment of "freeloaders." An expectation that government should make our lives better clashes with cynicism about the willingness or ability of government to accomplish anything constructive. Consciousness of harder economic times does not displace the deeply held conviction that anyone can make it if they really try. And running through it all, in the minds of most Americans, is the notion that many—perhaps most—of the poor are undeserving. In sociologist Mark Rank's study of welfare in Wisconsin, possibly his most discouraging finding came when he surveyed welfare recipients about their views of why they and others are on welfare. Rank asked whether recipients believed they were solely responsible for being on welfare, whether it was due to circumstances beyond their control, or some combination of the two. Speaking of themselves, 82 percent of the recipients blamed circumstances beyond their control, 12 percent cited a combination, and 6 percent took full responsibility. But 90 percent of these *welfare recipients* stated that, in general, "people on welfare" are partially or fully to blame for their situation. In short, even most welfare recipients themselves classify other recipients as undeserving.[11]

The result of this strong streak of blame is that public opinion victories tend to be narrow and fragile. In the campaign against the 1995 Personal Responsibility Act, the fight for public opinion was critical in securing President Clinton's veto of the legislation. But what apparently tipped the balance was not the National Welfare Rights Union's street actions, or the National Organization for Women's rally in Washington that categorized welfare cuts as violence against women, or even the *New York Times* ad by the feminist Committee of One Hundred Women, which declared that "a war against poor women is a war against all women!" Instead, a leak of the Clinton administration's own internal estimate that the law would plunge one million children into poverty, and a media push focusing on children spearheaded by the Children's Defense Fund and the National Association of Social Workers, finally achieved a Clinton veto. Of course, concern with the plight of children is an entirely appropriate reason to reject punitive welfare reform proposals. But focusing on children alone minimizes the simultaneous assault on the rights of women and poor people, leaving the door open for policies that control and punish women "for the sake of the children." As the Welfare Warriors of Milwaukee, Wisconsin, wrote in an angry 1995 open letter, "It is time for our allies to do more than apologize for our existence. It is time to stand up for our right to public support for our children and our right to mother our own children."[12] The narrowness of the 1995 veto victory became fully apparent the following year, when Clinton, finely attuned to election-year public opinion, signed a nearly identical welfare reform bill into law.

In future attempts to move public opinion, the tools currently used will remain important. There is an ongoing need for publications put out jointly by recipients and advocates, such as Boston's *Survival News* and Milwaukee's *Welfare Mothers' Voice*; supportive op ed articles and *New York Times* ads; cable television talk show appearances; and speaking tours by activists. But many of these media preach mostly to the converted, while potential allies turn the page or flip the channel. If we acknowledge that the battle for public opinion is actually more like a war of position, we must find ways to use the equivalent of both artillery and house-to-house combat.

The "big guns" consist of advertising, particularly on television and radio. When Republican New York Governor George Pataki announced a budget featuring $4 billion in cuts in February 1995, a coalition of unions, students, seniors, and others launched a grassroots campaign of lobbying and protest. But at the same time, unions and various institutional interests, such as hospitals and home care associations, spent several million dollars on an advertising blitz. Negative ratings of Pataki's performance rose from 38 percent to 63 percent; 65 percent of survey respondents said the budget fight made them "think less of the Republican Party of New York generally."[13] Of course, advertising takes money, so poor people can only pursue this strategy if they find allies with deep pockets—unions and churches being two key examples.

As for "house-to-house combat," this translates into one-on-one and small group discussion and education. The issues surrounding welfare are complex; soundbites cannot adequately capture them. Winning support for a full women's equality agenda means challenging deeply held beliefs about family, work, and government, while tapping into and nurturing other, equally deep beliefs—working through the contradictions we presented at the beginning of the book. Many forums are possible for this kind of discussion: house meetings, churches and other places of worship, PTAs, unions—wherever people live, work, and socialize. Mobilizing the people power for this kind of effort is even more difficult than mobilizing the millions of dollars needed for advertising campaigns, but without this nitty-gritty educational process, any leverage over public opinion will remain weak.

Putting it all together

Workplace organizing, conventional politics, protest, and campaigns to influence public opinion form a unified package. None of them will work well without all of the other elements. Furthermore, all of them require building new alliances and strengthening old ones. As with every major advance for women's economic equality in the past, broad coalitions uniting disparate interests will make the difference. We must overcome the divisions of class, race, and gender that have kept so many of us working at cross-purposes. It can be done.

And it has to be done. The costs and inefficiencies in our current system are keeping many people in this country down. The burden of childrearing is left to individual families, a larger and larger percentage of whom cannot find the time or money to do it well. Meanwhile, many families in dire poverty are trapped in unsafe neighborhoods, and a generation of children is growing up with little or no vision of a viable economic future. The costs of poverty, injustice, and inequality corrode the social fabric—sometimes sparking short-term explosions like urban riots, but more important, leading to long-term social polarization and decay. Taking into account how costly our current system has become and who is bearing that expense, the new costs of fixing the system are a good investment.

We all deserve a better society: one where women and men receive equal treatment, where employers and the government recognize family needs, and where poverty is replaced by opportunity. Equality for women and a better life for families of all kinds hang in the balance. It's time to smash those glass ceilings and banish those bottomless pits!

Notes

1. This discussion of strategy draws greatly on two excellent pieces on political strategy for welfare rights: Mimi Abramovitz, *Under Attack, Fighting Back: Women and Welfare in the United States* (New York: Monthly Review Press, 1996), part 4; Ann Withorn, "The Politics of Welfare Reform: Knowing the Stakes, Finding the Strategies," *Resist,* vol. 5, no. 3 (April 1996). In discussions of past political battles, we also draw on the essays in Louise A. Tilly and Patricia Gurin, eds., *Women, Politics, and Change* (New York: Russell Sage Foundation, 1990). We also thank Ann Withorn, Diane Dujon, and members of the Boston-area Academics' Working Group on Poverty for their helpful discussions.

2. Abramovitz, op. cit. This four-part approach to strategy borrows from the Detroit-based National Welfare Rights Union (NWRU), although we have set a somewhat broader agenda (since the target we focus on goes beyond welfare rights to encompass women's economic equality in general). In 1994, NWRU proposed a four-part strategy involving organizing, legislation, public relations, and legal strategy to combat the wave of punitive welfare "reforms" sweeping the country.

3. Ruth Milkman, "Gender and Trade Unionism in Historical Perspective," in Tilly and Gurin, op. cit.

4. Withorn, op. cit.

5. Nancy F. Cott, "Across the Great Divide: Women in Politics Before and After 1920," in Tilly and Gurin, op. cit.

6. This history of protest is based primarily on Abramovitz, op. cit., who provides much more detail than is presented here.

7. Welfare Mothers' Voice, "Fighting Back: Welfare 'Reform'—JEDI Women Spark Protests in 76 Cities," *Works in Progress* (Applied Research Center, Oakland, CA), April 1995: 6.

8. Kate Williams, "From the Streets . . . ," posting on the WELFAREM-L listserver (welfarem-l@american.edu), March 3, 1997. Original source appears to be Kensington Welfare Rights Union.

9. Barbara J. Nelson, "The Gender, Race, and Class Origins of Early Welfare and the Welfare State: A Comparison of Workmen's Compensation and Mother's Aid," in Tilly and Gurin, op. cit., and Linda Gordon, *Pitied But Not Entitled: Single Mothers and the History of Welfare* (New York: The Free Press, 1994).

10. Michael B. Katz, *The Undeserving Poor: From the War on Poverty to the War on Welfare* (New York: Pantheon, 1989).

11. Mark R. Rank, *Living on the Edge: The Realities of Welfare in America* (New York: Columbia University Press, 1994).

12. Welfare Warriors, "An Open Letter from Welfare Warriors to Friends of Families Who Receive Welfare Child Support," *Works in Progress* (Applied Research Center, Oakland, CA), April 1995: 7.

13. Labor Research Association, "Case Study in the New Politics," *LRA's Economic Notes* (May 1995): 3.

More Detailed Definitions of Family Types and Income Categories

Our classifications of seven mutually exclusive family types and five broad categories of income are discussed briefly in Chapter Three. This appendix provides a fuller account of both family types and income sources.

Family types

In order to discuss the myriad of diverse households in a way that is both comprehensive and comprehensible, we defined seven types of families. The family classifications are based on what we feel are the most salient characteristics for thinking about gender and income today: the number of adults, the presence of children, and the age and gender of the head of the household.

In this appendix, we fill out some of the differences among the family classifications.

Families with two or more adults.   Two of our family categories contain two or more adult family members. One contains related children under the age of eighteen, and the other does not. In the latter case we limited consideration to families whose head is under sixty-five years old. The vast majority of these families are married couples. Ninety-one percent of heads of two-or-more-adult-with-children families are married, compared to 85 percent of heads of such families without children.

Single-parent families.   These family types contain one adult of any age who lives with one or more related children under the age of eighteen. A small percentage (3 percent) of heads of these families are married, but their spouses are absent. Nineteen percent of single-mother families and 50 percent of single-father families live in households with other people to whom they are not related. Of these single parents living in households with unrelated others, large majorities (79 percent of single mothers and 90 percent of single fathers) live with one other family headed by someone of the opposite sex—in most cases, in fact, a family of one person of the opposite sex. It is reasonable to assume that many—probably most—of these households represent unmarried couples, but we have no way to tell lovers from roommates for either opposite-sex pairs or same-sex pairs. So we have stuck with a cautious definition of families that only includes persons related by birth, marriage, or adoption.

Lone adults.   These "families of one" are households in which an adult under the age of sixty-five lives without any other family members. The majority are people who have never been married—54 percent of the women and 61 percent of the men. Fifty-three percent of the men and 43 percent of the women live in households with other, non-related people. Of those living in households with non-related people, just over half are living with one family headed by someone of the opposite sex and just over one-quarter live with one family headed by someone of the same sex. Again, many of these pairs are probably more than just roommates, but we have not tried to guess about whether they share income, relying instead on our narrow definition of families.

Families with head sixty-five years or older.   We limit this category to families with no children under the age of eighteen in them; 44 percent consist of married couples. Of those who are not married, 37 percent are women who live alone and 12 percent are men who live alone (or with people unrelated to them), and the remaining 7 percent are men and women sixty-five and older who live with at least one other family member.

Income sources

Wages and salaries.   This category includes three types of earnings: wages, salaries, and self-employment income. Wages and salaries consist of the total money earnings received for work performed as an employee during the year, including Armed Forces pay, wages, salaries, commissions, tips, and cash bonuses earned before deductions are made for taxes, union dues, or pensions. Self-employment income consists of the net money income (gross receipts minus expenses) from one's own business, professional enterprise, partnership, or farm (as an owner, renter, or sharecropper). This value can be negative if expenses exceed receipts. In 1993, 75 percent of families had wages and salaries, and 10 percent reported self-employment earnings (positive or negative). The highest amount of income from this source that the Census Bureau will report for a family is $389,961 and the lowest value for self-employment income is a loss of $389,961.

Government transfers.   This category includes income received from the federal, state, or local government, except for government employees' pensions. There are four broad classes of benefits:

1. Social Security (OASDI): Social Security pensions and survivor's benefits, as well as permanent disability payments made by the Social Security Administration.
2. Supplemental Security Income (SSI): Payments made by federal, state, and local welfare agencies to low-income persons who are sixty-five years old and over, blind, or disabled.
3. Public Assistance: This includes Aid to Families with Dependent Children (AFDC) and state programs that have replaced it, as well as General Assistance.
4. Other: This includes unemployment compensation, veteran's payments, and workers' compensation from public and private insurance companies (when insurance is paid by the employer).

Table A.1 lists the average amount of income from each government source for each type of family.

Pensions and property income. This includes all pension income and income that derives from ownership of tangible and intangible property (except capital gains income, which is not recorded in Current Population Survey data). Pension income includes both private and government pensions and annuities, as well as disability and survivor income from insurance policies paid by employees. Property income includes interest, dividends, rental income, royalties, and income for estates or trusts. In 1993, the average amount of pension income received by all families was $1,353. Elder families were the family type with the highest average amount of this type of income ($4,131), while single mothers had the least ($39). The average amount of property income was $2,033. Again, families whose head was sixty-five or older had the highest average income from this source ($4,272), while single mothers had the lowest average amounts ($328).

Interfamily transfers. This income category includes money received in the form of alimony, child support, and other regular financial assistance from relatives or friends.

Other income. This includes income such as educational benefits and all other income not included in other categories.

Table A.1 Average Amount of Government Income by Type of Family, 1993

Type of government income	2 or more adults (under 65), no children	2 or more adults, with children	Head 65 and older, no children	Single mother	Single father	Lone female	Lone male
Social Security benefits	$1,265	$655	$9,081	$552	$482	$465	$317
Survivor's benefits	227	180	787	58	41	203	69
Permanent disability	236	115	97	56	41	67	108
SSI	145	168	192	231	79	181	136
Public assistance	38	252	14	1,418	243	61	34
Unemployment	338	338	49	138	263	161	245
Veteran's payments	154	81	271	27	53	38	103
Worker's compensation	143	183	55	44	178	48	124
TOTAL	$2,546	$1,970	$10,547	$2,525	$1,380	$1,223	$1,136

Note: Numbers in a single column may not exactly add up to the total due to rounding.

Source: Calculated by authors from U.S. Bureau of the Census, Current Population Survey, March 1994.

Women and Welfare:
Popular Conceptions vs. Facts

by Dorothy K. Seavey

Popular Conceptions	Facts
Benefits	
Cash welfare benefits constitute an adequate income for welfare recipients, giving them little incentive to work.	In 1996, the maximum monthly AFDC grant for a 3-person family in the median AFDC state was $389, or 36% of the 1996 federal poverty level.[1] [AFDC refers to the Aid to Families with Dependent Children Program, which was replaced by the Temporary Assistance to Needy Families (TANF) block grant in 1997.]
Welfare benefits have been increasing.	Over the period from 1970 to 1994, the median decline in real AFDC benefit levels was 47%.[1]
Welfare benefits may be declining, but together with in-kind benefits they constitute a generous package.	For a family with no income, the basic assistance package consists of AFDC, Food Stamps, and Medicaid.
	• In 1996, the combined maximum AFDC and Food Stamp grant for a family of 3 in the median AFDC state was $699 per month, or $8,388 per year, an amount that

189

Popular Conceptions	Facts
	was 35% below the federal poverty line of $13,267. Only 11 states had combined AFDC and Food Stamp benefits above 75% of the poverty threshold.[1]
	• Over the period from 1972 to 1993, the combined value of AFDC and Food Stamp benefits decreased by 27%, after adjusting for inflation.[1]
	• While Medicaid is an important part of the assistance typically provided to a family on AFDC, these benefits are not very fungible. They cannot be used to pay rent or purchase food or other necessities, and treating them as part of family income can have the perverse effect of making sick people look better off than healthy people.[2]
	• Food Stamps and Medicaid aside, other forms of assistance are either considerably smaller or received by only a minority of AFDC recipients, or both. For instance, in 1995, less than one-fourth (23%) of all AFDC families received any type of federal housing subsidy; the remaining 77% of AFDC families, although eligible for housing assistance, sought housing in the private market.[3]
Welfare recipients freeload on government programs while everyone else works hard to earn a living.	For many poor families, welfare assistance serves as de facto temporary disability insurance, unemployment insurance, and child support. Government assistance is not unique to families receiving welfare.
	• Over half of U.S. families receive government transfer payments from programs including Social Security ($352.1 billion), Medicare ($195.1 billion), unemployment compensation ($24.9 billion), agricultural price supports ($7.8 billion), federal employee retirement and disability payments ($43.8 billion), military personnel retirement and disability payments ($28.9 billion), and veterans' benefits and services ($16.2 billion).[4] (Figures are projections for 1996 federal outlays.)
	• In 1996, federal tax credits, exclusions, preferential tax rates, and deductions saved Americans tax expenditures of $3 billion on child and dependent-care expenses, $6.2 billion on capital gains (excluding agriculture, timber, iron ore, and

Popular Conceptions	Facts
	coal), $17.9 billion on deferral of capital gains on home sales, and $54.2 billion on mortgage interest on owner-occupied homes.[4]

Costs and Caseloads

Popular Conceptions	Facts
Welfare spending is out of control, and means-tested entitlement programs in general are burdening taxpayers and enlarging the federal deficit.	• In 1994, state and federal governments spent $25.9 billion on AFDC benefits and program administrative expenses. AFDC, as a share of federal spending, declined from 1.5% in 1975 to 1% in 1994, and, in the latter year, constituted only 5.7% of total federal spending on cash and noncash benefits for persons with limited income. AFDC accounted for less than 3% of the average state budget in 1995.[1]
	• During the 1980s, the percentage of the general population receiving AFDC averaged 4.5%. It increased to 5.4% by 1993, and then fell back to 4.6% in 1996.[1]
	• In 1994, combined federal spending on the AFDC population through the AFDC, Food Stamp, and Medicaid programs totaled roughly $50 billion, or about 3% of federal spending and 6% of federal social welfare expenditures. In comparison, federal outlays for national defense totaled $282 billion.[1,4]
Welfare caseloads have risen dramatically since the mid-1970s.	All increases in AFDC caseloads since the mid-1970s have occurred during recessions.[1] Between 1972 and 1990 welfare caseloads stayed roughly constant, fluctuating between 10.3 and 11.5 million recipients per month (or about 3.7 million families). With the recession of the early 1990s, unemployment rose, but fewer unemployed people were eligible for unemployment compensation. The number of average monthly AFDC recipients climbed to 13.6 million in 1992 and 14.1 million in 1993. In 1994, the caseload was 14.2 million (or 5 million families). By October 1996, the number of people receiving AFDC had dropped to 11.8 million.

Popular Conceptions	Facts
Family Characteristics	
Welfare primarily supports minority families.	In 1995, 31% of children who received AFDC were white, 39% were African American, and 22% were Hispanic.[3] Since 1973, the percentage of white families on AFDC had increased slightly, while the percentage of African American recipients had decreased and that of Hispanics had increased.[1]
Families receiving welfare are very large.	The size of the average family receiving AFDC in 1993 was slightly smaller than that of the average family in the general population—2.9 vs. 3.16 persons. Average AFDC family size had declined from 4.0 persons in 1970.[1] In 1995, about three-quarters (73%) of all families on AFDC had only 1 or 2 children, and almost 90% had 3 or fewer children.[3]
Most welfare recipients are able-bodied adults who have fallen into dependency and do not want to work.	• Welfare is primarily a children's program: in 1995, 69% of AFDC recipients were children, and 82% of these were under age 12. Fully 100% of adult welfare recipients care for children, nearly always without a spouse's assistance.[3] • Many adult welfare recipients are active in the labor market and are often part of the working poor. Research indicates that during the mid-1980s, 40% of adult AFDC recipients worked at paid jobs, either simultaneously combining work and welfare or cycling between the two. Nearly three-quarters (71%) of recipients had recent work histories.[5]
Welfare today exclusively supports children born out of wedlock and women who don't marry their children's father.	In 1995, 14% of recipient children had an unemployed, incapacitated, or deceased parent; 25% had parents who were divorced or separated; and 57% had unmarried parents.[3] The proportion of women on AFDC who had never married more than doubled since the mid-1970s, increasing from about one-fifth to one-half.[6]

Popular Conceptions	Facts
	However, the growth in never-married women who are mothers has been greater among women who are not welfare recipients. The proportion of these mothers in the general population tripled between 1976 and 1992, increasing from 12% to 36%.[4,6]

Teen Mothers

Popular Conceptions	Facts
There is an epidemic of teen childbearing in the United States.	Each year, about 11% of all females aged 15-19 become pregnant, and approximately 13% of all births are to teens. Teen births have been declining over the last thirty years. In 1970, women under 20 had 656,460 babies; by 1995, that number had dropped to 513,062. In 1955, there were 90 births per 1,000 females aged 15-19; this rate fell to 50.2 in 1986, and then rose to 62.1 by 1991. Since the early 1990s, the teen birth rate has been declining, reaching 56.9 in 1995.[7]
Teenagers account for most unplanned pregnancies and out-of-wedlock births.	Adult women, not teenagers, account for large majorities of the unintended pregnancies, abortions, and nonmarital births that occur each year. Only about 25% of all unplanned pregnancies each year occur to teenagers.[8] Seven in 10 births to teenagers occur outside marriage, yet adolescents account for a smaller proportion of all nonmarital births today (31%) than they did in 1970 (50%).[7]
Teen parents are better off living with their parents.	For many pregnant and parenting teens, "home" may not be a safe place. Studies indicate that the majority of teen parents have been sexually and/or physically abused as children.[9]
Most teen mothers are African American.	The majority of teen mothers are white. In 1995, 70% of teens giving birth were white and 27% were black. Hispanics account for an increasing percentage of teen

Popular Conceptions	Facts
	births, increasing from 13% in 1985 to 24% in 1995. (Hispanic persons may be of any race.)[7]
Welfare encourages adolescent mothers to establish independent households, and most teen mothers are heading households alone.	According to data from the mid-1980s, most teen mothers (4 out of 5) live with relatives, usually parents, and sometimes with husbands, but not by themselves. More black than white adolescent mothers live with relatives. Only 15% of white and 12% of black adolescent mothers were single and living alone with their children.[10]
Most welfare recipients are teen mothers.	Few welfare recipients are teen mothers: in 1995, only 6% of adult female AFDC recipients were age 19 or younger.[3]
Teen mothers inevitably end up on welfare.	Data from 1986 and 1987 indicated that nearly 50% of teen mothers entered welfare within 5 years of giving birth. About half of single teen mothers left AFDC within one year and almost three-quarters left within 3 years. However, women who gave birth as teenagers are disproportionately represented among those recipients who remained on AFDC for long periods.[10]
Welfare encourages teen childbearing.	Research suggests that adolescent childbearing and mothering by low-income teenagers reflect an interrelated complex of factors, including the availability of employment and career opportunities, school performance, self-esteem, childhood sexual victimization and abuse, and sexual pressures and coercion by adults. This research also suggests that economic self-sufficiency is problematic for many teens at risk of early childbearing, no matter how long they delay motherhood.[11]

Popular Conceptions	Facts
Birth Trends	
The welfare system has fueled a dramatic increase in out-of-wedlock childbearing.	Research has generally shown that AFDC benefit levels have had no effect, or only a small effect, on birth rates for unmarried women.[12] The trend toward increased non-marital childbearing is a society-wide phenomenon that is not exclusively concentrated among the poor or the less educated but reflects changing reproductive and marital behavior at all ages and income levels.[6]
Child exclusion policies that deny benefits for children born into a family on welfare are needed to curb out- of-wedlock births.	• Child exclusion policies are based on unsupported assumptions and ignore the complex reasons that women have children. There is so far no research evidence that lowering grant levels will result in lower birth rates to welfare mothers.[13] • The average family receiving welfare has less than 3 children; the size of families receiving welfare has decreased, not increased, over time;[1] and having additional children while receiving welfare is not a lucrative venture.
Reducing Dependency	
Most people on welfare get trapped in the system and stay on for years as welfare becomes a way of life.	The typical pattern of welfare receipt is not one of long-term continuous receipt. There appears to be considerable flux back and forth between low-wage work and AFDC. • Monthly data indicate that, of all people entering the AFDC program, 56% left within 1 year and 70% left within 2 years. Only 18% stayed on continuously for more than 5 years.[14] • About half of those who exited left for employment. The majority of these, however, ended up returning (most within 2 years), often because of a lack of stable employment and inadequate or unaffordable child care or health insurance.[14]

Popular Conceptions	Facts
	• While welfare as a way of life was not the reality for most AFDC recipients, there was a significant minority which received benefits for extended periods: of women beginning a first AFDC spell, a third accumulated total time on welfare of 7 years or more. A significant proportion of these longer-term recipients also moved on and off welfare, unsuccessful in their efforts to leave welfare permanently.[15] • Growing evidence suggests that domestic violence is highly prevalent among women receiving welfare and can create serious impediments to moving toward economic self-sufficiency, particularly within a structure of strict time-limited welfare.[16]
Paid employment is the solution to welfare dependency. Jobs are available and chances are good that families on AFDC can move out of poverty if they would just work more.	• An increasing number of jobs pay low earnings. Over the period from 1973 to 1995, the share of workers with annual earnings lower than the poverty level for a 4-person family increased from 24% to 30%.[17] Furthermore, women are much more likely than men to earn poverty-level wages.[17] • Real wages for workers in the bottom fifth of the wage distribution fell 11.1% from 1979 to 1995.[17] Despite overall low unemployment rates in 1996, one-fifth of black women were unemployed and more than one-third were underemployed. The rates are slightly lower for Hispanic women (16% and 29%).[18] • In recent years, the minimum wage has dropped to a near 40-year low when adjusted for inflation. Legislation enacted in 1996 to raise the minimum wage to $5.15 an hour by September 1997 will make up some of the decline due to inflation during the 1980s, but by 2000 the wage will still be 26.7% below its 1979 level.[17]

Popular Conceptions	Facts
	• Other characteristics of many low-wage jobs that create obstacles to relying on paid employment for economic self-sufficiency include the short duration and high turnover of many of these jobs; deteriorating job mobility prospects within and across firms; the increasing incidence of part-time and temporary work; inadequate or nonexistent nonwage compensation (e.g., health insurance); and ineligibility for unemployment insurance coverage.[19]
A strict time limit is needed to move families off welfare.	Imposing an arbitrary time limit disregards what research data show about how families use welfare, the type of employment available to low-wage female workers, and the heterogeneity of the welfare caseload. AFDC entry and exit rates suggest that a high proportion of recipients are unable to leave welfare permanently with one employment-induced exit, or within a 2-year time period, and that high rates of job loss constitute substantial obstacles to successful welfare-to-work transitions.[14,15,20] The challenge is not to force families to stop using welfare, or to require more recipients to enter employment, but rather to make paid work a viable alternative. This requires addressing the employment barriers faced by low-income women, as well as creating low-wage jobs that are bridges to better-waged employment.
Welfare is a way of life passed on within families from generation to generation, creating intergenerational welfare dependency.	Research indicates that 75% of welfare recipients did not grow up in welfare households. Growing up in a household that receives public assistance does increase the likelihood of welfare receipt, but this is the result of the impact of economic background, not parental welfare use, on the prospects of children who grow up in families with limited resources and opportunities.[21]

Sources

1. Committee on Ways and Means, U.S. House of Representatives (1996) *1996 Green Book: Overview of Entitlement Programs*. Washington, DC: U.S. Government Printing Office; National Association of Child Advocates (1996) *Ready, Willing, and Able: What the Record Shows About State Investments in Children, 1990-1995*. Washington, DC: National Association of Child Advocates; Congressional Research Service, Washington, DC (1996 data on monthly AFDC and Food Stamp grants from CRS telephone survey).
2. Citro, Constance F. and Robert T. Michael, Eds. (1995) *Measuring Poverty: A New Approach*. Washington, DC: National Academy Press.
3. Administration for Children and Families (1995) *Characteristics and Financial Circumstances of AFDC Recipients: FY 1995*. Washington, DC: U.S. Department of Health and Human Services.
4. Bureau of the Census (1996) *Statistical Abstract of the United States: 1996*. (116th edition) Washington, DC: U.S. Government Printing Office.
5. Spalter-Roth, Roberta, Beverly Burr, Heidi Hartmann, and Lois Shaw (1995) "Welfare That Works: The Working Lives of AFDC Recipients." Washington, DC: Institute for Women's Policy Research.
6. General Accounting Office (1994) "Families on Welfare: Sharp Rise in Never-Married Women Reflects Societal Trend." May, GAO/HEHS-94-92, Washington, DC: GAO.
7. Ventura, S.J., J.A. Martin, and S.M. Taffel *et al.* (1994) "Advance report of final natality statistics, 1992." *Monthly Vital Statistics Report* October 25, Vol. 43, No. 5, Supplement, Hyattsville, MD: National Center for Health Statistics, U.S. Department of Health and Human Services; National Center for Health Statistics (1996) "Births and Deaths in the United States, 1995." *Monthly Vital Statistics Report* October 4, Vol. 45, No. 3, Supplement 2, Hyattsville, MD: National Center for Health Statistics, U.S. Department of Health and Human Services.
8. The Alan Guttmacher Institute (1995) "Teen Age Pregnancy and the Welfare Reform Debate." *Issues in Brief* February, New York and Washington, DC: Guttmacher Institute.
9. Boyer, Debra and David Fine (1992) "Sexual Abuse as a Factor in Adolescent Pregnancy and Child Maltreatment." *Family Planning Perspectives* Vol. 24, No. 1, January/February, pp. 4–11; Roper, Peggy and Gregory Weeks (1993) "Child Abuse, Teenage Pregnancy and Welfare Dependency: Is There a Link?" October, Olympia, WA: Washington State Institute for Public Policy.
10. Congressional Budget Office (1990) "Sources of Support for Adolescent Mothers." September, Washington, DC: CBO.
11. Landry, David J. and Jacqueline Darroch Forrest (1995) "How Old Are U.S. Fathers?" *Family Planning Perspectives* July/August, Vol. 27, No. 4, pp. 159–161; Boyer, Debra and David Fine (1992) "Sexual Abuse as a Factor in Adolescent Pregnancy and Child Maltreatment." *Family Planning Perspectives* Vol. 24, No. 1, January/February, pp. 4–11; Roper, Peggy and Gregory Weeks (1993) "Child Abuse, Teenage Pregnancy and Welfare Dependency: Is There a Link?" October, Olympia, WA: Washington State Institute for Public Policy; McCrate, Elaine (1992) "Expectations of adult wages and teenage childbearing." *International Review of Applied Economics* Vol. 6, No. 3, pp. 309–328; Jacobs,

Janet L. (1994) "Gender, Race, Class, and the Trend Toward Early Mother-hood." *Journal of Contemporary Ethnography* January, Vol. 22, No. 4, pp. 442–462; Abrahamse, Allan F., Peter A. Morrison, and Linda J. Waite (1988) "Teenagers Willing to Consider Single Parenthood: Who Is at Greatest Risk?" *Family Planning Perspectives* Vol. 20, No. 1, January/February, pp. 13–18.

12. Moffitt, Robert (1992) "Incentive Effects of the U.S. Welfare System: A Review." *Journal of Economic Literature* March, Vol. 30, pp. 1–61; Danziger, Sheldon et al. (June 23, 1994) "Researchers Dispute Contention That Welfare is Major Cause of Out-of-Wedlock Births," Ann Arbor, MI: School of Social Work, University of Michigan.

13. Nightingale, Demetra (1992) "Assessing the Impact of Recent AFDC Proposals Addressing Family Behavior." June 26, Mimeo. Paper prepared for Children's Roundtable on Welfare Reform and the Family; Donovan, Patricia (1995) "The 'Family Cap': A Popular But Unproven Method of Welfare Reform." *Family Planning Perspectives* July/August, Vol. 27, No. 4, pp. 166–171.

14. Pavetti, LaDonna (1993) "The Dynamics of Welfare and Work: Exploring the Process by Which Women Work Their Way Off Welfare." Ph.D. dissertation, Harvard University.

15.   Bane, Mary Jo and David T. Ellwood (1994) *Welfare Realities: From Rhetoric to Reform*. Cambridge, MA and London: Harvard University Press.

16. Allard, Mary Ann, Randy Albelda, Mary Ellen Colten, and Carol Cosenza (1997) *In Harm's Way? Domestic Violence, AFDC Receipt, and Welfare Reform in Massachusetts*. February, Boston, MA: McCormack Institute and Center for Survey Research, University of Massachusetts-Boston.

17. Mishel, Lawrence, Jared Bernstein, and John Schmitt (1996) *The State of Working America: 1996–97*. Armonk, NY and London: M.E. Sharpe.

18. Bernstein, Jared (1997) "The Challenge of Moving from Welfare to Work." Mimeo, Washington, DC: Economic Policy Institute.

19. Seavey, Dorothy K. (1996) *Back to Basics: Women's Poverty and Welfare Reform*. Special Report CRW 13, Wellesley, MA: Wellesley College Center for Research on Women.

20. Berg, Linnea, Lynn Olson, and Aimee Conrad (1991) "Causes and Implications of Rapid Job Loss Among Participants in a Welfare-to-Work Program." Evanston, IL: Center for Urban Affairs and Policy Research.

21. Rank, Mark R. and Li-Chen Cheng (1995) "Welfare Use Across Generations: How Important Are the Ties That Bind?" *Journal of Marriage and the Family* August, Vol. 57, pp. 673–684.

General Resources: Child Welfare League of America (December 1994) "Welfare Reform: Myths vs. Facts." Washington, DC; Teresa Amott (November 1994) "Welfare Myth vs. Reality." Lewisburg, PA: Bucknell University, Department of Economics; Diana Pearce and Emily Knearl (February 1994) "Teen Pregnancy, Welfare, and Poverty: Myths vs. Facts." Washington, DC: Women and Poverty Project, Wider Opportunities for Women; Children Now (December 1994) "Myths and Facts About Welfare Families in the US." Oakland, CA; Center on Social Welfare Policy and Law (1996) *Welfare Myths: Fact or Fiction?* New York, NY.

C

Resources

Guide to National Organizations and Resource Centers

9 to 5 Working Women's Education Fund

614 Superior Ave. NW
Cleveland, OH 44113
414-274-0933

- Conducts research on the concerns of women office workers.

American Federation of Labor and Congress of Industrial Organizations (AFL-CIO)

815 Sixteenth Street NW
Washington, DC 20006
202-637-5000
http://www.aflcio.org

- The nation's main federation of unions, representing millions of workers. Conducts organizing, research, education, and advocacy on labor issues.

American Federation of State, County and Municipal Employees (AFSCME)

1625 L Street NW
Washington, DC 20036
202-429-1000
http://www.afscme.org/afscme/
   pol-leg/welftc.htm

- Major union of state and local public employees. Web site includes resources on welfare reform (laws and documents, links to federal and state information, etc.)

Association of Community Organizations for Reform Now (ACORN)

739 8th Street SE
Washington, DC 20003
202-547-9292
http://www.acorn.org/community/

- Advocates for local involvement and control over issues affecting communities.

"Benefice" network of nonprofit organizations

http://www.benefice.com/html/
search.cgi

• Directory of about 2,400 nonprofit organizations, with phone numbers, directors, goals, and objectives. Many of the groups deal with women's and children's welfare.

Center for Community Change

1000 Wisconsin Avenue, NW
Washington, DC 20007
202-342-0519
tomkinst@com.change.org

• Helps local groups run by low-income people to organize themselves and their communities, build affordable housing, and develop successful issue campaigns.

Center for Law and Social Policy (CLASP)

1616 P Street NW, Suite 150
Washington, DC 20036
202-328-5140
http://www.clasp.org

• Conducts research and policy analysis on issues affecting low-income families.

Center for Third World Organizing

1218 East Twenty-First Street
Oakland, CA 94604
510-533-7583
http://www.ctwo.org

• National organization dedicated to the struggle for social and economic justice for low-income people and people of color.

Center on Budget and Policy Priorities

820 First Street NE, Suite 510
Washington, DC 20002
202-408-1080
http://www.cbpp.org

• Provides research and information on federal and state government funding programs that affect low- and moderate-income people. Conducts special studies on minorities and poverty.

**Center on Social Welfare Policy and Law
(Welfare Law Center)**

275 Seventh Avenue, Suite 1205
New York, NY 10001
212-633-6967
hn1035@handsnet.org
http://www.afj.org/

• A national legal and policy organization that focuses on means-tested cash public assistance programs. Provides representation for poor people in litigation and before administrative and legislative bodies and analysis of developments in welfare law, training, and individualized assistance for local welfare advocates.

Child Care Law Center

22 Second Street, Fifth Floor
San Francisco, CA 94105
415-495-5498
info@childcarelaws.com

- Monitors legislation that relates to child care issues. Provides training, technical assistance, and legal services to advocates working on behalf of child care for low-income families.

Children's Defense Fund

25 E Street NW
Washington, DC 20001
202-628-8787
http://www.childrensdefense.org/

- Provides research, advocacy, public education, written materials, monitoring of federal agencies, assistance to state and local groups, and community organizing on a wide range of issues that affect children and youth.

Coalition on Human Needs

1000 Wisconsin Avenue NW
Washington, DC 20007
202-342-0726
HN0079@handsnet.org

- An alliance of over 100 national organizations working together to promote public policies that address the needs of low-income and other vulnerable Americans. Promotes adequate funding for human needs programs, progressive tax policies, and other federal measures, and serves as an information clearinghouse.

Electronic Policy Network

http://epn.org/index.html#text/

- A project of *The American Prospect* (a liberal journal), this Web site provides access to *The American Prospect*, *Political Science Quarterly*, and a variety of liberal policy institutes and foundations, including the Economic Policy Institute and Families USA. Includes resources on welfare at http://epn.org/idea/welfare.html

Fairness and Accuracy in Reporting (FAIR)

130 West Twenty-fifth Street
New York, NY 10001
212-633-6700
http://www.fair.org/fair/

- A media-watch organization advocating pluralism in media. Maintains a speaker's bureau, compiles statistics, and publishes a magazine.

HandsNet

http://www.handsnet.org

- A national, nonprofit organization that promotes information sharing and advocacy among individuals working on a broad range of public interest issues, focusing on human services. One feature at this Web site is Welfare Reform Watch, which covers current welfare reform efforts at the national, state, and local levels.

Institute for Research on Poverty

University of Wisconsin Madison
1180 Observatory Drive
3412 Social Science Building
Madison, WI 53706
608-262-6358
http://www.ssc.wisc.edu/irp

- Organizes academic research conferences and publishes papers on all aspects of poverty.

Institute for Women's Policy Research

1400 Twentieth St. NW, 104
Washington, DC 20036
202-785-5100
http://www.iwpr.org

- Researches economic issues important to women and families, including low-wage work, poverty, welfare reform, child care, family leave, contingent work, pay equity, and healthcare. Maintains a computer listserver on welfare reform, WELFAREM-L.

Jobs with Justice

501 Third St., NW
Washington, DC 20001
202-434-1106
http://www.igc.org/jwj/

- A national campaign for workers' rights; local chapters include coalitions of religious, labor, and community organizations active throughout the country.

Joint Center for Political and Economic Studies

1090 Vermont Ave, NW,
   Suite 1100
Washington, DC 20005
202-789-3500

- Through research and information dissemination, aims to improve the socioeconomic status of black Americans, increase their influence in the political and public policy arenas, and facilitate the building of coalitions across race lines.

Joint Center for Poverty Research (Northwestern University/ University of Chicago)

2046 Sheridan Road
Northwestern University
Evanston, IL 60208-4108
847-491-4145
http://www.spc.uchicago.edu/
    wwwuser/orgs/povcen/

• Organizes academic research conferences and publishes papers on all aspects of poverty. Focuses on the causes of poverty and the effectiveness of policies aimed at reducing poverty.

Low Income Housing Coalition

1012 Fourteenth Street NW,
    Suite 1200
Washington, DC 20005
202-662-1530

• Educates the public and organizations about low-income housing through conferences, publications, and technical assistance.

National Association for the Advancement of Colored People (NAACP)

1025 Vermont Ave, NW,
    Suite 1120
Washington, DC 20005
202-638-2269
http://www.naacp.org/

• Works to achieve equal rights through the democratic process and to eliminate racial prejudice by removing discrimination in housing, employment, voting, education, the courts, transportation, recreation, and business.

National Association of Community Action Agencies

1100 17th Street, NW
Washington, DC 20036
202-265-7546
http://www.nacaa.org/

• National association of federally funded local anti-poverty agencies. Resources include information about the National Dialogue on Poverty.

National Association of Neighborhoods

1651 Fuller Street NW
Washington DC 20009
202-332-7766

• National Association of Neighborhoods is a national umbrella organization for community-based organizations and small businesses. It currently includes a membership of 2,000 organizations and businesses in 38 states. These groups engage in local activities designed to enhance the quality of life in neighborhoods through social and economic change.

National Center for Children in Poverty

Columbia University
154 Haven Avenue
New York, NY 10032
212-304-7100
http://cpmcnet.columbia.edu/ dept/nccp/

• Conducts research and education on children in poverty.

National Coalition for the Homeless

1612 K Street NW, Suite 1004
Washington, DC 20006
202-775-1322
http://nch.ari.net

• Provides information and education to people and organizations working with the homeless and promotes housing for low-income families.

National Council of La Raza

1111 Nineteenth St. NW,
Suite 1000
Washington, DC 20036
202-310-9000
http://www.nclr.org

• National umbrella organization working for civil rights and economic opportunities for Latinos.

National Jobs for All Coalition

475 Riverside Drive, Room 853
New York, NY 10115
212-870-3449
http://www.igc.apc.org/esp/
   njfac.htm

• Dedicated to providing jobs with sufficient pay for all who want them and to demonstrating the linkages between unemployment and other problems facing the nation, such as women's rights, the environment, and economic justice.

National Organization for Women

1000 Sixteenth Street NW,
   Suite 700
Washington, DC 20036
202-331-0066
http://www.now.org

• Works to end discrimination and gender inequality in all facets of life and to increase the number of women elected to political office. Open to all who support gender equality.

National People's Action/ National Training and Information Center

810 North Milwaukee Avenue
Chicago IL 60622-4103
312-243-3038 (NPA),
312-243-3035 (NTIC)
hn1742@connectinc.com

• National People's Action is an activist congress of over 300 neighborhood and community organizations. The National Training and Information Center provides technical assistance, training, consulting, and research to neighborhood leaders and groups, and informs grassroots groups on a variety of issues, including community reinvestment, affordable housing, anti-crime and -drugs, affordable energy, jobs/small business creation, and health care.

National Radio Project

830 Los Trancos Road
Portola Valley, CA 94208
415-851-7256
http://www.igc.apc.org/
  MakingContact/

• Devoted to airing popular and progressive voices in the media. Broadcasts a weekly radio show entitled Making Contact that focuses on current issues; available free to every public radio station in the U.S. and Canada.

National Rainbow Coalition

1700 K Street NW, Suite 800
Washington, DC 20006
202-728-1180

• Encourages the development of a progressive political leadership dedicated to economic justice, peace, and human rights.

National Urban League

500 East Sixty-second Street
New York, NY 10021
212-310-9000
http://www.nul.org

• Works for racial equality for African-Americans and other minorities in all phases of life. Fights institutional racism and provides direct service to minorities in the areas of employment, housing, education, social welfare, health, law, consumer rights, and community and minority business development.

Poverty & Race Research Action Council

1711 Connecticut Ave. NW,
  Room 207
Washington, DC 20009
202-387-9887
prrac@aol.com

• Funds research that is linked to organizing and advocacy on issues of poverty and race.

Russell Sage Foundation

112 East Sixty-fourth St.
New York, NY 10021
212-750-6000
http://epn.org/sagehtml

• Funds research on work, income inequality, and poverty. Publishes working papers and books on these and related topics.

Service Employees International Union

1313L Street, NW
Washington, DC 20006
202-637-5000
http://www.seiu.org

• One of the nation's largest public employee unions. Active in organizing low-wage workers, and concerned about welfare in part because its members include human service workers.

Urban Institute

2100 M Street, NW
Washington, DC 20037
202-833-7200
http://www.urban.org

• Liberal research institute that conducts research on public policy issues including poverty, inequality, and racial discrimination.

Welfare Information Network

1000 Vermont Ave. NW, Suite 600
Washington, DC 20005
202-628-5790
welfinfo@welfareinfo.org
http://www.welfareinfo.org/

• Works as a clearinghouse for information, policy analysis, and technical assistance on welfare reform.

Wider Opportunities for Women

815 Fifteenth Street, NW,
   Suite 916
Washington, DC 20005
202-638-3143
vstaples@w-o-w.org

• Works nationally and locally to achieve economic independence and equality of opportunity for women and girls. Provides organizing, skills training, and technical assistance for women workers.

Guide to Government and Statistical Resources on the Internet

American Public Welfare Association—Welfare News in the States

http://www.apwa.org/statenew/textonly.htm

• State-by-state descriptions of welfare reform initiatives.

Children's Defense Fund—Selected Features of State Welfare Plans

http://www.childrensdefense.org/stateplans.html

• Profiles state welfare plans.

Government Information Sharing Project—USA Counties 1996

http://govinfo.kerr.orst.edu/usacostateis.html

• Provides a Web interface to U.S. county-level Census data. Includes poverty data by race, age, and family composition.

Local Government Home Page

http://www.localgov.org

- Links to the official home pages of many city and county governments.

National Association of Counties

http://www.naco.org

- Information gathered by county-level governments. Includes National Internet Clearinghouse, http://www.naco.org/nich/index.htm, which provides links to state legislation, court cases, local actions, and news stories.

National Association of State Information Resource Executives

http://www.nasire.org

- Represents information resource executives and managers from the fifty states, six U.S. territories, and the District of Columbia. Warning: Information is not always kept up to date. Particular resources of interest include StateSearch (subject directory for state government information): http://www.nasire.org/ss/

National Association for Welfare Research and Statistics

http://ucdata.berkeley.edu/NAWRS/index.html

- NAWRS aims to promote and exchange ideas for the betterment of research and statistics in the field of public welfare.

National Center for Children in Poverty State Reports

http://cpmcnet.columbia.edu/dept/nccp/state/state0000.html

- Reports on the availability of support services for children by state.

National Conference of State Legislatures—Welfare Reform Connection

http://www.ncsl.org/statefed/welfare/welfare.htm

- Provides information about state and federal actions and analyses of key welfare issues.

National Governor's Association—Welfare Reform

http://www.nga.org/welfare/

- Includes state information on welfare reform and links to states' home pages on welfare reform. Resources of particular interest include:

    Summary of recent developments:
        http://www.nga.org/welfare/WelfareRecentDevelopments.htm
    Matrix of components in state welfare reform plans:
        http://www.nga.org/welfare/WelfareDocs/MatrixAndTANFSumry.htm

THOMAS: Legislative Information on the Internet

http://thomas.loc.gov

- This site carries the full text of major legislation passed in recent Congresses.

U.S. Census Bureau

http://www.census.gov/

- All the Census Bureau publications are available through their WWW site, including statistical abstracts, housing and household economic statistics, income inequality, income statistics and poverty graphs. Particular resources of interest include:

CenStats (includes all Census publications since January 1, 1996):
http://www.census.gov/mp/www/index2.html
Housing statistics: http://www.census.gov/hhes/www/index.html
Income and poverty estimates at state and county levels:
http://www.census.gov/hhes/www/saipe.html
Income inequality: http://www.census.gov/hhes/www/incineq.html
Income statistics: http://www.census.gov/hhes/www/income.html
Maps: http://www.census.gov/datamap/www/index.html
Poverty statistics: http://www.census.gov/hhes/www/poverty.html
Statistical Abstract (1996 compendium of statistical tables):
http://www.census.gov/prod/2/gen/96statab/96statab.html

U.S. Department of Health and Human Services

Administration for Children and Families
http://www.acf.dhhs.gov/

- The federal agency that administers Temporary Assistance to Needy Families (the main welfare program for poor single mothers). Includes a link to welfare reform information. Resources include links to state welfare, children, and families Web pages at http://www.acf.dhhs.gov/news/welfare/stlinks.htm

U.S. Federal Government Agencies Page

http://www.lib.lsu.edu/gov/fedgov.html

- Provides access to the Web sites of most federal agencies, organized by Executive, Judicial, Legislative, Independent, Boards, Commissions and Committees, and Quasi-Official.

Welfare Reform Bill of 1996: HR3734, Personal Responsibility, Work Opportunity, and Medicaid Restructuring Act of 1996

http://libertynet.org/~edcivic/iscvhome.html

- This World Wide Web site offers direct and easy access to the complete text version of the bill as passed.

Guide to Frequently Published
Research Materials

Dollars and Sense. Bimonthly popular economics magazine. Frequently covers issues of poverty and inequality. November/December 1996 issue was a special issue on welfare reform. Subscriptions or single copies available from 1 Summer Street, Somerville, MA 02143, 617-628-8411, email dollars@igc.apc.org.

Focus. A quarterly publication of the Institute for Research on Poverty, featuring research summaries. Free. Can be requested directly from the Institute (listed above).

Green Book, or *Background Material and Data on Major Programs within the Jurisdiction of the Committee on Ways and Means* (of the U.S. House of Representatives). The best source of detailed information on major federal entitlement programs. Available from U.S. Government Printing Office (GPO), Superintendent of Documents, Stop SM, Washington, DC 20402. To order materials from the GPO call 202-512-1800 or fax to 202-512-2250. Also available through their WWW site at http://www.gpo.gov

Insight & Action; The Human Needs Report. A bimonthly newsletter and legislative update published by the Coalition on Human Needs (listed above).

Money Income in the United States (Current Population Reports, Series P-60). (Title sometimes varies.) Annual summary of income data for households, families, and individuals in the United States, based on a survey of one in 1,000 families. Issued by the Census Bureau. Available from U.S. Government Printing Office or through their web site at http://www.gpo.gov. Much of the information is also available at the Census web site at http://www. census.gov/hhes/www/ income.html

Poverty in the United States (Current Population Reports, Series P-60). (Title sometimes varies.) Annual summary of poverty data for households, families, and individuals in the United States (including official poverty rates), based on a survey of one in 1,000 families. Issued by the Census Bureau. Available from U.S. Government Printing Office or through their web site at http://www.gpo.gov. Also available at the Census web site at http://www. census.gov/hhes/www/poverty.html

Poverty & Race. Contains topical articles as well as listings of recent reports and meetings. Published six times a year by the Poverty & Race Research Action Council (listed above).

Poverty Research News. A quarterly publication of the Joint Center for Poverty Research, featuring research summaries. Free. Can be requested directly from the Joint Center.

Statistical Abstract of the United States. The best source of general economic data. Published annually by the U.S. Bureau of the Census. Available from the Government Printing Office (GPO), Superintendent of Documents, Stop SM, Washington, DC 20402. To order materials from the GPO call

202-512-1800 or fax to 202-512-2250. You can also access the materials on U.S. Bureau of the Census's homepage at http://www.census.gov

Survival News. Grassroots welfare rights newspaper published by recipients. C/o Betty Reid Mandell, 102 Anawan Avenue, W. Roxbury, MA 02132, phone 617-327-4219.

Update. Lists the most recent developments in welfare issues. Published by the Center for Law and Social Policy (listed above; *Update* is also available at http://www.clasp.org). Number of issues per year varies. Subscriptions also include their quarterly newsletter, *Family Matters*.

Welfare News. Tracks recent legislative developments. Published by the Center on Social Welfare Policy and Law (listed above).

The information in this section was compiled by Elissa Braunstein of the Center for Popular Economics (Amherst, MA) and Urska Cvek of the University of Massachusetts at Lowell, in addition to the authors. An expanded list appears in Randy Albelda, Nancy Folbre and the Center for Popular Economics, *The War on the Poor: A Defense Manual* (New York: The New Press, 1996). Some information in this section is based on Carolyn A. Fisher and Carol A. Schwartz, eds. *Encyclopedia of Associations 1996*, 30th ed. (New York: Gale Research Inc., 1995), and on Barbara Burg, "Welfare: No Scarcity of Resources on Web," *Nieman Reports*, Spring 1997, 38-42.

Index

A

Abramovitz, Mimi, 90

adults, family of two or more: effectiveness of anti-poverty policies, 82-3, *82*, 85; income sources, 38, *38-9*, 40, 41, *42-3*, 43-4; in-kind benefits to, 88; population percentage, *35*, 36; poverty rates, *36-7*, 37, 43-4, *43*, 134; *see also* families

adults, lone: effectiveness of anti-poverty policy on, *82*, 83; income sources, *38-9*, 41, *42-3*, 43-4; in-kind benefits to, 88; population percentage, 34, *35*, 36; poverty rates, *36-7*, *43*, 44; *see also* families

affirmative action, 15, 46

AFL-CIO, 167, 168

African Americans, *see* blacks

ages: and income potential, 35, *35*; poverty rates by, 26-8, *27-9*, 36-7, *36-7*, 94, *94*

Aid to Families with Dependent Children (AFDC): benefit levels, decreasing, 98, 99, 101-2, 109-10, 135, *136-7*; benefit levels, inadequacy of, 13, 72-4, *73*; birthrates and receipt of, 68,

69, 99, 116-17; expenditure amounts, 96, 100, 101, 124; job training programs, 60-1, 109, 110, 118-19, 121, 124, 127; origins, of, 91; program termination, 122-3; as unemployment insurance, 112, 156; who receives, 12, 40, 68, 70-1, *71*, 122, 126; *see also* welfare

Aitcheson, Susan, 155

Alabama, welfare policies, 69

alimony, as income, 40, 41, *42-3*

American Enterprise Institute, 97

American Federation of State, County, and Municipal Employees (AFSCME), 168

anti-poverty policies: behavior-based (victim-blaming), 96-7, 97-100, 115-18; devaluing childcare, 13, 14, 118; economic growth theory, 91-5; effects of, by family type, 82-5, *82*, *84-5*; history of, 89-91; ineffectiveness of, 13, 79-85, *80-2*, *84*, 101-2; marriage as, 68, 90, 116, 144; poverty measurement techniques affecting, 21; *see also* welfare reform

Aronson, Joshua, 99

Page numbers in italics refer to tables or figures on those pages.

214   Glass Ceilings and Bottomless Pits

Asian Americans, poverty rates, 24, *24-5, 28,* 83
AT&T, downsizing, 51

B
Bailyn, Lotte, 152
Baltimore, MD., training program, 110
The Bell Curve (Herrnstein & Murray), 98
birth rates, and receipt of welfare, 14, 68, 69, 99, 116-17
blacks: poverty rates, 24, *24-5,* 28, *28,* 30, 83; poverty relief discrimination, 90, 91; single mothers, 66, 70, 83; stereotypes of, 30; unemployment rates, 50-1; wage discrimination, *53,* 54, 70; women in paid labor force, 3-4; *see also* race and ethnicity
Blank, Rebecca, 85, 86
block grants: for childcare, 60, 124, 151; origins of, 96; state control of, 108, 123-5, 139; *see also* Temporary Assistance to Needy Families (TANF)
Bridefare, 116
Butler, Stuart, 99

C
Canada, anti-poverty policies, 69, 79-81, *80-1, 84,* 85
cash entitlements, *see* Aid to Families with Dependent Children (AFDC); Supplemental Security Income (SSI); *see also* social security, unemployment insurance
Census Bureau, U.S.: defining families, 33-4; poverty data, 20, 23, 86, 87
Center for Budget and Policy Priorities, 125
central-city poverty rates, 24, *24-5,* 26, *28,* 30, 70
Chavez-Thompson, Linda, 168

child allowances, 16, 140; in Europe, 148
childcare: block grants, 60, 124, 151; costs of, 21, 56-7, *57-8, 73;* devaluation of, 8-9, 11, 13-14, 118; European subsidized programs, 149; limitations on work, 4-5, 13-14, 51-6, *52-3,* 59-60, 70-1; national policies lacking for, 60, 61-2; proposal for system of assistance, 15, 150-1; provisions during training/employment, 60-1, 126-7, 137-9, 140, 141, 142; tax credits for, 60, 150-1; time requirements, 13-14, 59-60, 61-2, 70-1, 111
children: benefits cut to, 102, 115, 116, 127, *136-7,* 178; community responsibility for, 11, 150, 161; effects of poverty on, 68, 70; health care costs for, 56; poverty rate of, 8, 23, *24-5, 28-9, 94; see also* families
child support: from deadbeat fathers, 14, 41, 113-15, 139-40; European policies, 148, 151; income received from, 40-1, *42-3, 73,* 114-15; insurance, 139-40; limits placed on, 102, 115, 139; orders, 140
clerical jobs, 45, *49,* 66; union organizing of, 167-8
Clinton, Bill (William J.), 96, 158, 177-8
college education: affordability, 157-9; child support payments and, 115; effects on wages, 6, 46, *46;* poverty and, 26, *26-7;* as welfare component, 141-2; welfare reform and, 119
Committee on National Statistics, 22
communities: coalitions with labor unions, 169; economic development by, 16, 159; responsibility for children by, 11, 150, 161
comparable worth, *see* pay equity

Page numbers in italics refer to tables or figures on those pages.

Page numbers in italics refer to tables or figures on those pages.

Page numbers in italics refer to tables or figures on those pages.

About South End Press

South End Press is a nonprofit, collectively managed book publisher with more than 180 titles in print. Since our founding in 1977, we have tried to meet the needs of readers who are exploring or are already committed to the politics of radical social change.

Our goal is to publish books that encourage critical thinking and constructive action on the key political, cultural, social, economic, and ecological issues shaping life in the United States and in the world. In this way, we hope to give expression to a wide range of democratic social movements and to provide an alternative to the products of corporate publishing.

Through the Institute for Social and Cultural Change, South End Press works with other political media projects—*Z Magazine*; Speak Out, a speakers bureau; Alternative Radio; and the Publishers' Support Project—to expand access to information and critical analysis.

For a free catalog, please write to South End Press, 116 Saint Botolph Street, Boston, MA 02115; call 1-800-533-8478; or visit our website at http://www.lbbs.org.

Other Titles of Interest

For Crying Out Loud: Women's Poverty in the United States
Diane Dujon and Ann Withorn, eds.

Regulating the Lives of Women: Social Welfare Policy from Colonial Times to the Present
Mimi Abramovitz

Race, Gender, and Work: A Multicultural Economic History of Women in the United States
Teresa Amott and Julie Matthaei

Chaos or Community? Seeking Solutions, Not Scapegoats for Bad Economics
Holly Sklar

About the Authors

RANDY ALBELDA (left), Associate Professor of Economics at the University of Massachusetts–Boston, is co-author of *The War on the Poor*.

CHRIS TILLY, Associate Professor of Policy and Planning at the University of Massachusetts–Lowell, is author of *Half a Job: Bad and Good Part-Time Jobs in a Changing Labor Market*.

Together, they serve on the editorial collective of *Dollars & Sense* magazine, and have written extensively on the connections among poverty, family structure, and work. They have been active in local, state, and national campaigns on issues of welfare reform, women's equality, job quality, and fair taxes.